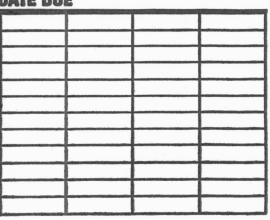

SOVIET POLITICS, 1945–53

SOVIET POLITICS, 1945–53

Timothy Dunmore
Lecturer in Government
University of Essex

St. Martin's Press   New York

© Timothy Dunmore 1984

Printed in Hong Kong
Published in the United Kingdom by The Macmillan Press Ltd.
First published in the United States of America in 1984

ISBN 0–312–74869–8

Library of Congress Cataloging in Publication Data
Dunmore, Timothy.
Soviet Politics, 1945–53.
Includes bibliographical references and index.
1. Soviet Union—Politics and government—1945–
2. Soviet Union—Economic policy—1946–1950. I. Title.
JN6511.D85   1984   947.084'2   83–40702
ISBN 0–312–74869–8

Contents

List of Charts

1 Soviet Politics in Stalin's Last Decade

INTRODUCTION

In September 1945 the Soviet Union emerged victorious but battered from its four-year war with Nazi Germany. Stalin's Russia lost twenty million dead and 128 billion dollars' worth of industrial capital in the conflict, but its losses were not only physical. In the face of a determined invader Stalin had had to liberalise many aspects of the political system he had built up in the 1930s. In Soviet culture during the war nationalist feelings were allowed to emerge; western influences and even religious sentiments were encouraged in order to spur on the war effort. On the economic front a degree of private enterprise, especially on the part of the collective farm peasantry, had to be encouraged to feed a starving population and army. The central political structures in Stalin's repressive system, the secret police and the Communist Party, found their roles redefined and the ranks of their membership diluted in wartime. In foreign policy Russia surrounded herself with a series of most unlikely capitalist allies. In terms of both policies and political structures the Soviet system had become markedly more liberal during the war.

This has led many to see the period immediately after the war until Stalin's death in 1953 in terms of a restoration of the policies and political discipline of the pre-war years. The various events associated with the *"Zhdanovshchina"* certainly lend much weight to this view. In the years 1946–48 there was certainly an attempt led by Andrei Zhdanov to eradicate wartime laxity in all the areas mentioned above. Discipline and central control were to be restored to cultural and foreign affairs, to the collective farms and the party.

Yet the emphasis of this book is to open up another side to the

1

politics of the immediate post-war years. The "clampdown" hypothesis outlined above interprets the period as one of Stalinist orthodoxy in which political decisions were made by Stalin and perhaps a few leading lights in the Politburo, and then were faithfully carried out by the Soviet state bureaucracy under the ever-watchful eyes of the party and police. This book, through a detailed study of the formulation and implementation of the major policy decisions of the time, shows how, on the contrary, these decisions were frequently the result of compromise between disputing factions inside and outside the leading Politburo and that all too often decisions that did not satisfy their implementors in the state and party apparatus were not carried out in the form prescribed. In other words it will be argued that policy making and implementation involved not just Stalin and a few cronies but also a wide circle of senior officials in the Soviet system.

The rest of this chapter is devoted to a discussion of the primary sources upon which this analysis of the post-war years is based, and to a brief overview of the various models of the policy-making process to be found in the voluminous literature on Soviet politics. Chapter 2 presents a guide to the structures of the Stalinist system as it emerged from the war and an assessment of their basic functions. In subsequent chapters the formation and implementation of policy in several distinct spheres is analysed, the major fields under discussion being industry, agriculture, foreign affairs and culture and ideology.

SOURCES

The study of Soviet politics under Stalin in both the 1930s and 1940s has been bedevilled by a shortage of primary sources upon which to base research. As Roger Pethybridge wrote,

> The last stage of Stalin's rule is as difficult to interpret as any period in the Middle Ages. The poverty of Soviet sources on this period contrasts with their unusual abundance, by Soviet standards, for the years after 1953.[1]

This is presumably the reason for the lack of studies of the 1940s in

the West. The only works in the English language devoted
entirely to the 1940s and early 1950s have either concentrated
heavily on foreign policy[2] or cultural policy[3] or have consisted
more of memoirs or biography than detailed analysis.[4] For the rest
one has to rely on a motley collection of chapters from books on
Soviet history, politics and economics, which, valuable though
they are, are limited in scope when applied to Stalin's last
decade.[5] The result, as Jerry Hough has observed, is that:

> For many younger students of the Soviet Union and for the vast
> majority of specialists on comparative government, all that has
> remained of the last decade of Stalin's regime have been
> generalisations embodied in the totalitarian model and in the
> comparative textbooks.[6]

This book relies heavily on the primary sources that many
assumed did not exist, were inaccessible to foreign scholars or
were simply not very informative. Soviet politicians, academics
and bureaucrats did put their views on policy issues on paper both
in the 1940s and after Stalin's death. In 1950 the Soviets
published 7831 different newspapers, 1408 journals and periodi-
cals and 40 000 books. In spite of the post-war shortage of
newsprint there existed ample means through which opinions and
views could be expressed in Stalin's Russia.

Only the quality of these sources remains to be questioned.
Stalin's Russia was not known for its toleration of divergent views.
Do Soviet writings from the 1940s therefore tell us anything of the
politics of the time? It is true that some authors and journalists
tended to avoid controversy by reiterating official decrees,
engaging in lengthy presentations of statistics or simply studying
remote historical periods. A leading economist noted in 1947 that:

> The scientific level of the books and brochures on the problems
> of the new Five Year Plan is, with rare exceptions, not high
> enough, and many of them are of no significant practical value.[7]

Yet there were sufficient exceptions to enable us to unravel
some of the policy debates that preceded Politburo decisions and
to examine the behaviour of Stalin's bureaucracy. This is
particularly true if we recognise the mode of political discourse
operative in Soviet politics at the time. Sidney Ploss has pointed

out that policy debates often take place in rather covert forms in the USSR. He identified what he called a "language of conflict"[8] by means of which officials and specialists in a particular field could air divergent views without appearing to the casual observer or the general public to do so. It is this detection of the actual opinions hidden behind a facade of public uniformity that has become known as "Kremlinology". Whilst the Kremlinological technique can be taken too far, its utility rests on the fact that many senior political figures in the USSR itself also "read between the lines" of official pronouncements and seemingly innocuous articles and books to seek out the political controversies of the time.

The language of conflict in use in the immediate post-war years had its own distinguishing features. Whilst in the 1950s Soviet authors might associate views with "certain comrades" to avoid mentioning names, in the preceding decade they often avoided even acknowledging their opponents' views! Public political arguments in the 1940s tended to run along parallel rather than conflicting lines, with one person advocating, for example, a concentration of industrial resources on the western areas of the USSR and another on the eastern regions, with neither admitting in print that the two views were mutually contradictory.

Another device in common use at the time was to criticise an individual or a particular case as a covert method of criticising a group of people or a widespread practice. An excellent illustration of this is given by Alex Inkeles' content analysis of readers' letters published in eight Soviet newspapers in 1947.[9] Such letters were often solicited by newspapers to publicise defects in the Soviet administration structure which affected the implementation of policy. The letters do not normally complain of *general* ineptitude (which might reflect badly on the system as a whole), but of apparently isolated cases in which particular officials had failed to implement Politburo decisions or were making it difficult for others to do so.

About two-thirds of the complaints analysed by Inkeles (which related to industrial matters) concerned the supply and utilisation of equipment and raw materials. Eighty-eight per cent of them were directed against the organs of the Council of Ministers and the Soviets, mostly the former. These complaints about shortcomings in the work of particular agencies in particular production units were a covert means of attacking more general malpractice on the part of the state bureaucracy. They reveal much about the implementation of policy decisions in Stalin's Russia.

A substantial amount of material about Stalin's last decade has also been published since his death. Discussion of this period in Soviet publications has been limited by the sensitivity even today of the "destalinisation" issue. Yet under Khrushchev's leadership some discussion of Stalin's role was allowed, most notably by Khrushchev himself in his "secret speech" of 1956 and later revelations both before and after his enforced retirement in 1964.[10] Other important political figures of the 1940s have also written valuable memoirs[11] or have been the subject of biographies published in the USSR.[12]

One of the most serious gaps in information about the Soviet Union published in the 1940s was the lack of comprehension and reliable statistics. The publication of many economic statistics was made illegal in 1947. Yet that deficiency has largely been made up since 1956 as series of statistical handbooks have been produced.[13] They cover not only the period from 1953 but also the preceding years. The data that was actually collected in the 1940s has now been published and even, in some cases, corrected to remove acknowledged distortions.[14]

The study of Stalin's last decade by both Western and Soviet scholars has become all the easier in recent years as the period has become more a part of the past and less related to current issues and personalities in Soviet politics. Many compilations of official resolutions and decrees from the period have been published in the USSR since the 1950s.[15] Some Soviet scholars have also been allowed to delve into the party and state archives of the time, although these still seem to be closed to Westerners. Nevertheless some very interesting material from these archives has been made available to us through the works of Soviet scholars, albeit in rather a piecemeal fashion.[16] In the last five years several works have been published in Britain and the USA making fuller use of these original materials.[17] As yet no attempt has been made to combine the fruits of these researches to produce a more comprehensive overview of the politics of post-war Stalinist Russia. It is hoped that this book will fill that gap.

From all these sources it is possible to reach a much more accurate assessment of the *modus operandi* of the Soviet political system in the years 1945 to 1953 than has yet been produced. One can only hope that the passage of time will allow yet more material to become less politically controversial in the USSR and to be made accessible to scholars. The demise of the current generation of political leaders should facilitate this. Many of the Brezhnev/Kosygin Politburo were deeply involved in the politics of the 1940s and would have no great wish to reveal that today. At least three of the Brezhnev leadership (Brezhnev, Kosygin and Suslov) were members of Stalin's Politburo!

MODELS OF THE SOVIET POLICY-MAKING PROCESS

Before embarking on a detailed analysis of the power structure of Stalinist Russia it is necessary broadly to define the yardsticks against which to assess that structure. A number of students of the Soviet polity have distinguished three distinct approaches to Soviet politics, what Tarschys calls the Totalitarian, the Bureaucratic and the Pluralist models.[18] The first sees the Soviet political process in centralised and repressive terms. The leadership (in our case Stalin and perhaps his Politburo) are basically responsible for policy decisions. They do not need to respond to pressures from below – from the bureaucracy or from the public – when they take their decisions. Their directives are unquestioningly implemented by a state bureaucracy constantly harassed by the leadership's agents, the party apparatus and the secret police.

The bureaucratic or organisational[19] model shifts the emphasis of political power from the Politburo to the bureaucracy. The main feature of the Soviet political process is seen as the role of the senior administrators in ensuring that policy decisions are carried out. In some conceptions this view takes the leadership's decisions as predictable, dictated by the official ideology of the regime.

The "input" side of the policy-making process, in which individuals and groups seek to pressure political leaders to pursue particular policies, is assumed by these two models to be insignificant in Stalinist Russia. The pluralist approach, on the other hand, emphasises the plurality of views and interests within the Soviet political and administrative hierarchy and sees decisions primarily as compromises between these different interests. In Rigby's terms, policies are the outcome of *bargaining* between groups and factions rather than the *fiat* of a dictator or an oligarchy.

This is not the place to enquire too deeply into the internal consistency of these models. The purpose of distinguishing the three approaches is to focus our analyses of the making of policy in various fields on seeking out the evidence which best fits each model. Each model has had many variations played upon it. We specify the most appropriate versions for Stalin's last decade and indicate what sort of evidence is required to substantiate them.

The original totalitarian theory was founded on the idea that Stalin exercised a "near total" political control over the whole of the USSR.[20] Later studies have, however, emphasised that there was some disagreement over policy within Stalin's Politburo.[21] This "conflict" model[22] limits the scope of policy debate to the party's Politburo and so takes account of the wranglings amongst Khrushchev, Malenkov, Andreev, Molotov and others that clearly affected policy-making in the 1940s.[23] If the conflict version of the totalitarian model is the most apt description of Soviet policy-making in the 1940s, then one would expect to find evidence of policy dispute only amongst Politburo members. In addition one would expect the orders of the Politburo to be executed reasonably faithfully by the bureaucracy.

The bureaucratic model really complements rather than contradicts the totalitarian model in that it assumes no significant political pressures on the Politburo's decision-making. In its more realistic variants this model does, however, admit that the directives and decrees issued by Stalin's Politburo were not always implemented as faithfully as the totalitarian theorists would have us believe.[24] Such non-fulfilment was not due to any refusal on the part of administrators to comply with the wishes of higher authorities, but rather to the fact that they could not possibly carry out all the orders they were given. The leadership tended to set tasks for the bureaucracy that were so difficult that they could not possibly complete them in full. All that was really expected was that the bureaucracy should do its best to ensure that the most important of those tasks were achieved. In the economic sphere, for example, a factory manager might be ordered to raise both the quality and the quantity of his output. Often a shortage of resources would prevent him achieving both and he would sacrifice quality for the sake of quantity. Provided he achieved the quantitative targets set by his superiors they would turn a blind eye to his failure to raise quality.

Under such circumstances some non-compliance with the leadership's wishes was inevitable but not significant. This type of bureaucratic model allows for the validity of the sort of complaints Inkeles analysed, but argues that the most important priorities of the leadership's policies were carried out by the bureaucracy.

The third model to be considered, the pluralist, is the only one to lay stress on the input side of the policy-making process. It suggests that policy decisions were made by the Politburo with due regard for the divergent views expressed by its numerous advisers and administrators. If opinions like these were put forward and did have an impact on Politburo decisions, then this model may be the more appropriate description of the Soviet policy-making process.

A further amendment might be made to the pluralist model to allow for the non-implementation of orders noted by the bureaucratic model. If this non-implementation was more organised, deliberate and biased in particular directions than bureaucratic theorists would allow, then even the leadership's basic priorities might not be achieved. One explanation of such a pattern might be in terms of the leaders' failure to consult the appropriate sections of the administration before determining those priorities. If the Politburo ignored some pluralist pressures at the input stage it might find the same pressures applied to it at the implementation stage. It needs to be shown whether Stalin's bureaucrats would carry out a policy to whose formulation they had not been a party and to whose principles they did not adhere.

An assessment of these three models of the Soviet political systems in the period after the war therefore must involve us in a detailed study of the formulation, decision and implementation of policies. Yet such a study should not be expected to bring us down on the side of only one model to the exclusion of the other two. Clearly all three have a grain of truth in them; some policy decisions were obviously affected by Politburo discussion and Stalin's personal intercessions; some administrators clearly neglected the fulfilment of some decrees in order to implement others; and there was some debate over policy matters outside the ranks of the Politburo. What this book sets out to examine is a matter of emphasis, whether policy outcomes were *more* the result of Politburo, bureaucratic or pluralist activity. In this task our approach is clearly coloured by the fact that the emphasis of previous writings on this period has been on the totalitarian side. This book seeks to redress the balance in favour of the pluralist and bureaucratic elements in the politics of Stalinist Russia.

2 The Soviet Power Structure, 1945–53

THE STRUCTURE

The Stalinist political system was a mass of complex bureaucratic structures and organisations with ill-defined functions and over-lapping responsibilities. The main barrier to an understanding of this system lies in the fact that the formal and legal roles assigned to institutions often did not indicate their real importance. This is nowhere clearer than in the cases of the Supreme Soviet of the USSR and the All Union Congress of the Communist Party. In theory these two bodies were representative of the masses of the people and the party respectively. In practice they met very rarely – the Soviet for a few days each year and the Congress only once between 1945 and 1953 – and they were largely ceremonial occasions. Real decision-making power lay to an extent with the executive bodies of the Soviet – the Council of Ministers and the the Presidium – but above all with the party's executive – the Politburo and Secretariat.

Chart 2.1 presents a simplified guide to the power relations of the Stalinist system. It cannot, however, do justice to its complexities. Besides the formal subordinate relationships indicated by the lines on the chart, there existed a wealth of informal contacts between organisations at all kinds of levels. It is these contacts that figure largely in the detailed analyses of subsequent chapters. The aim of this chapter is to delineate the functions of the main agencies and to assess the resources they had at their disposal to carry them out in the post-war years.

A crude division of functions between the Council of Ministers, the party and the Soviets and their subordinate organisations would run as follows. The party makes policy decisions, the Council of Ministers breaks these down into more detailed

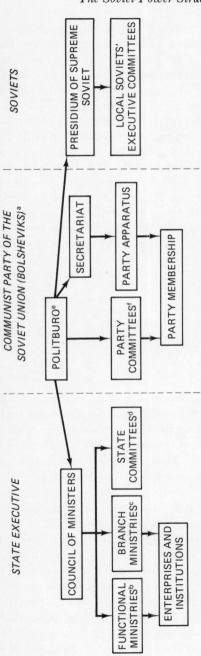

CHART 2.1　*The Stalinist power structure* (simplified)

SOVIETS

PRESIDIUM OF SUPREME SOVIET

LOCAL SOVIETS' EXECUTIVE COMMITTEES

COMMUNIST PARTY OF THE SOVIET UNION (BOLSHEVIKS)[a]

POLITBURO[e]

SECRETARIAT

PARTY APPARATUS

PARTY COMMITTEES[f]

PARTY MEMBERSHIP

STATE EXECUTIVE

COUNCIL OF MINISTERS

STATE COMMITTEES[d]

BRANCH MINISTRIES[c]

FUNCTIONAL MINISTRIES[b]

ENTERPRISES AND INSTITUTIONS

Notes

[a]　The more formal and ceremonial bodies such as the Supreme Soviet and the All-Union Party Congress, have been omitted for the sake of clarity.

[b]　e.g. Ministry of Finance, Ministry of Internal Affairs ⎱ renamed in April 1946 (previously

[c]　e.g. Ministry of Agriculture, Ministry of Higher Education ⎰ People's Commissariats)

[d]　e.g. Gosplan

[e]　Renamed Presidium October 1952 and membership enlarged.

[f]　Central Committee and Buros of Union republic party organisations, *obkomy* (provincial party committees), *gorkomy* (city party committees) and *raiskomy* (district party committees).

N.B.　Many of these bodies had equivalents at regional levels.

directives which it then carries out. The Soviets also have implementation functions in some policy spheres (such as housing) but their main role is in publicising and legitimising the Politburo's decisions. This simple picture, however, may hide almost as much as it reveals. Politburo decisions were not reached in a vacuum; it was the acknowledged responsibility of many state and party bodies, like Gosplan or the Departments of the party Secretariat, to provide the leadership with information and advice upon which to base its decisions. Further it was the task of nearly every subordinate agency to check that the Politburo's decisions were being carried out by the branch ministries. Bodies like the secret police and the Ministry of Finance under the Council of Ministers, the apparatus of the party and the committees and deputies of Soviets were all supposed to check on (*kontrolirovat'*) the activities of these implementing ministries. This was also one of the functions of some of the hierarchies that would not be considered part of the power structure in some countries, notably the Soviet trade union organisation.

THE DECISION-MAKERS

There can be little doubt that most of the authoritative pronouncements on policy in the forties emanated from Stalin and his Politburo. Whether they were dressed up as decrees of the Supreme Soviet or resolutions of the party's Central Committee, they were Politburo decisions. That does not mean that these decisions did not reflect opinion outside the Politburo. It does mean, however, that an understanding of the role and functioning of Stalin and his Politburo is crucial to an analysis of the politics of the post-war years.

The view of Stalin's relationship with his Politburo colleagues that is presented by many observers is one of a master and his servants. For example, Milovan Djilas, the Yugoslav communist who visited the USSR in 1947, describes Molotov (a senior Politburo member) following Stalin around with a small notebook in his hand taking down the dictator's every wish.[1] Khrushchev describes how meetings of the Politburo were called at Stalin's convenience, usually at his country house and often at one or two o'clock in the morning.[2] In the early 1950s Stalin is supposed to have excluded Molotov, Voroshilov and Mikoyan from Politburo meetings by the simple expedient of not inviting them![3] Khrushchev further told a 1963 session of the party's Central Committee that Stalin presented an economic plan to the Politburo for its approval but refused to let the meeting actually see the plan![4]

These anecdotes are apparently backed up by the fact that Stalin had gone to great extremes in the 1930s to remove all challenges to his power as General Secretary of the party and thus dictator of the USSR. Having murdered his contemporary rivals Bukharin, Trotsky and Kirov, was not Stalin head and shoulders above his colleagues in the 1940s in terms of political power and experience? Yet the Politburo of the 1940s was by no means full of young aspiring politicians who owed their positions solely to Stalin and had had no experience of Soviet politics before the purges of the 1930s. Men like Andreev, Voroshilov, Molotov, Mikoyan and Kaganovich had been members of the Politburo since the early or mid-1920s, that is since long before the final expulsion of either the left or the right opposition from the party. Of the 11 members of the 1947 Politburo, four had been appointed to it in 1926 and two (Molotov and Stalin himself) even earlier. This is not to say that these men were not loyal to Stalin, but that Stalin perhaps could not remove them at will. That could explain why Stalin excluded Molotov, Voroshilov and Mikoyan from meetings rather than simply having them arrested and shot.

There can be no doubt that Stalin was the most important figure in the Politburo, but his colleagues had their own power bases and Stalin had to rely on them to a degree for information and advice. This was particularly so in view of the dictator's advancing years and ill health. However fit and able he was, one man would find it very difficult to keep control of the affairs of a country of 150 million inhabitants. When that man was seventy years old, as was Stalin in 1949, and not in the best of health, his reliance on others must have been that much greater. Roy Medvedev, the Soviet dissident historian reveals that "Decrepitude marked the last years of Stalin's life, following his seventieth birthday in 1949."[5] His public appearances were very few and far between at this time. After his election speech in Moscow in February 1946 Stalin made only one more speech in public, at the 19th Party Congress in 1952. Then he spoke only for five minutes or so and his performance was obviously something of an ordeal for him. After about 1946 he ceased to attend many important ceremonial occasions, such as the annual parades to celebrate the October revolution.

Not only was Stalin ill for much of his last decade, he also became something of a recluse obsessed with relatively unimportant matters at the expense of rather more weighty issues of policy. Medvedev makes the latter point this way:

> In the last years of his life Stalin began to display a characteristic of many monarchs, neglect of affairs.[6]

In the immediate post-war years, until about 1949, Stalin devoted much of his attention to foreign affairs at the expense of domestic. In his last four or five years he seems to have spent more time on writing books on economics and linguistics than on involving himself in the details of running a country.

Long before this Stalin had exhibited a tendency to isolate himself from his people and to rely on others for information about the state of the nation. Khrushchev bluntly stated:

> Stalin did not like the people. When did he ever visit factories? Probably the last occasion was his visit to the Dinamo plant in 1924. After that he went almost nowhere.[7]

and that Stalin

> . . . knew the country and agriculture only from films, and these films had dressed up and beautified the existing situation in agriculture.[8]

Alexander Werth, a journalist in the USSR at this time, wrote that:

> People who were well acquainted with Stalin and his immediate entourage have told me in recent years a great deal about the way in which he became an "angry old man" at some time during 1948 or 1949. During the greater part of these two years and right up to his death in 1953, he was seldom in Moscow. He lived nearly all the time at his government *dacha* at Kuntsevo, and governed, as it were, mostly by proxy.[9]

In summary, for much of his last decade Stalin was neither capable of managing nor interested in many spheres of policy. He therefore had to rely on his senior Politburo colleagues to provide him with information (which they often doctored to suit their own ends), to carry out his wishes, and even to take the decisions for him. It seems unlikely that any of the Politburo would have gone directly against Stalin's wishes, but they certainly struggled with each other to influence the dictator and to present him with a set of ready-made decisions for his approval.

The key to an understanding of Stalin's post-war Politburo lies in knowledge not only of the dictator's physical and mental health, but also of the quarrels over policy that divided various factions within it. Stalin did little to discourage these disputes by dismissing or eliminating the participants, either because he did not wish to or even because he could not do so.

Stalin's Politburo quarrelled over foreign policy, cultural policy, and agricultural and industrial matters.[10] In the early post-war years the major issues revolved around the aggressiveness of Soviet foreign policy, the cultural "hard line" of the *Zhdanovshchina* and industrial policy. In all these spheres the hard line was associated with what William McCagg calls the "party revivalist" faction led by Zhdanov. After Zhdanov's death (from natural causes) in 1948 it was the opposing Malenkov–Beria faction, with its support in the state bureaucracy, that came more to the fore. Stalin probably brought Khrushchev to Moscow from the Ukraine to counter the power of this faction. In the early 1950s Khrushchev and Malenkov were at loggerheads over various agricultural matters.

Even if Stalin wanted to suppress these disputes he found it very difficult to do so. His practised method of resolving conflicts was to have one side or another removed. Yet there were no dismissals from the Politburo after the war until 1949. Then Nikolai Voznesensky was arrested and executed. Over the last few years of Stalin's life only two members of the Politburo were demoted, G.M. Popov and A.A. Andreev, and neither was arrested. Indeed both remained in responsible positions in the Soviet hierarchy. McCagg argues persuasively that Stalin was unable to limit the power of the Malenkov–Beria faction after Zhdanov's death.[11] In spite of attempts (like the "Mingrelian Affair")[12] to purge their supporters the "dictator" could not directly attack their power positions. There is some evidence that Stalin was planning a purge in 1953 to cut the ground from under their feet. His death prevented this purge from mushrooming into a threat to Politburo members. The fact that he had to resort to the devious means he had used in 1934 to remove his colleagues is indicative of the weakness of his position in 1953. In 1934 Stalin had probably arranged the murder of his rival Kirov and then blamed it on many other enemies who were subsequently purged. In 1953 he accused several Kremlin doctors of seeking to murder leading political figures as a means of starting off a similar purge amongst the Malenkov–Beria faction.

Stalin's relative weakness at this time may have owed something to the entrenched positions of many of his colleagues as well as to his own incapacity. The power of the Malenkov–Beria axis was based on the support enjoyed by the former amongst senior officials in the economic ministries and the latter amongst secret police officials and party leaders in his native Caucasus. Similarly Zhdanov had relied for his position partly on the support of leading figures in the party apparatus whose role in both domestic and foreign affairs he sought to enhance in his "party revival". The logic behind these statements is that Politburo members relied on the support of party and state officials *outside* the Politburo as well as on the goodwill of Stalin himself. As Stalin's capacity declined so these other supports became more important in the struggle for influence over policy decisions within the Politburo.

The support a Politburo member had was often related to the policy sphere for which he was responsible. Within Stalin's leadership each person was in charge of a particular sphere of policy or region of the country. Chart 2.2 shows the responsibilities, formal and informal, of the Politburo and the Party Secretaries in 1947. This system of policy "overlords"[13] often involved an individual holding a variety of offices at the same time. For example, in 1950 G.M. Popov was at one and the same time a Central Committee Secretary, secretary of both city and *oblast'* (provincial) party organisations in Moscow, and Minister of Urban Construction. That meant that he was in charge of the post-war rebuilding of Moscow. At a lower level it was very common for the same person to head the party organisations of a town and the surrounding *oblast'* (province) or republic of the USSR.

These "overlords" were held responsible for their own policy

	Official post	Sphere of de facto responsibility
1 Full members of Politburo		
Stalin J.V.	General Secretary CC CPSU and Chairman CM	
Molotov V.M.	DC CM; Min. Foreign Affairs	Foreign Affairs
Malenkov G.M.	DC CM	Industry
Zhdanov A.A.	Secretary CC CPSU	Cultural and Party Affairs
Beria L.P.	DC CM	Police
Andreev A.A.	DC CM; Chairman Party Control Commission. Chairman Council on Kolkhoz Affairs	Agriculture
Voznesensky N.A.	DC CM; Chairman State Planning Committee	Planning
Khrushchev N.A.	1st Secretary and Chairman CM, of Ukraine	Ukraine
Voroshilov K.E.	DC CM and Chief Allied Control Commission in Hungary.	Military (Abroad)
Mikoyan A.I.	DC CM and Min. of Foreign Trade	Foreign Trade
Kaganovich, L.M.	DC CM; Min. of Construction Materials	Construction
2 Candidate members		
Bulganin N.A.	DC CM & Min. of Armed Forces	Military (in Russia)
Kosygin A.N.	DC CM	Light Industry
Shvernik N.M.	Chairman Supreme Soviet Presidium	Soviets
3 Central Committee Secretaries		
Kuznetsov A.A.	Secretary CC CPSU	Police
Popov G.M.	Secretary CC CPSU and 1st Secretary Moscow Party	Moscow
Patolichev N.A.	Secretary CC CPSU and Deputy Chairman of Council on Kolkhoz Affairs	Agriculture
Pegov N.M.[a]	Secretary CC CPSU	Party Organs

NOTES
CC   Central Committee
CM   Council of Ministers
DC   Deputy Chairman
Min. Minister

[a] It seems that Pegov took over Patolichev's place as a party secretary but not his agricultural portfolio. He probably took over many of Andreev's duties as Chairman of the Party Control Commission, leaving him free to concentrate on agricultural affairs and ending any duplication of responsibilities in the Politburo and Secretariat.

CHART 2   *The responsibilities of the Politburo and Secretariat, 1947* areas or regions and that has led some to argue that they were "little Stalins" who ignored the wishes of their subordinates but could be removed by Stalin himself if anything went wrong in their sphere. There is, however, a wealth of evidence that these little Stalins did respond to some extent to their subordinates and, further, that Stalin was not able to transfer or dismiss his overlords at will. Beria remained in charge of police affairs throughout the period 1945–53 and Malenkov in overall control of industrial affairs for the same period; Alexei Kosygin was the overlord for consumer goods industries for most of Stalin's last decade. Stalin did manage to transfer a number of his colleagues to new responsibilities, but only after 1949 and particularly in the shakeup of October 1952, just six months before his death.[14] This degree of security of tenure suggests that Stalin could not easily dismiss his overlords; it also implies that they in turn had to build up contacts and loyalties amongst their immediate subordinates. It is the impact of many of these subordinates and leadership factions on the Politburo's decisions that will be analysed in subsequent chapters.

In summary Stalin's relations with his Politburo were not simply those of an autocrat and his minions. Like an absolute monarch Stalin needed his courtiers to act as his eyes and ears and even his brain. One could, however, go further than this and suggest that Stalin was not in full control of his "little Stalins" and that especially towards the end, one faction of the Politburo might have been powerful enough to frustrate his will, even when that will was expressed. It is no accident (as Stalin himself might have said) that Malenkov and Beria assumed the leading posts in the USSR immediately after Stalin's death. However this work will also examine the relevance of politics outside the Politburo in Stalin's Russia and it is to these structures that we now turn.

THE IMPLEMENTORS – THE BRANCH MINISTRIES

The final responsibility for the implementation of Politburo decisions in most policy spheres rested with the ministries. Only in matters of ideology and social security were the party and the trade unions (respectively) concerned with the direct implementation of decisions. Their major task was to check on and coordinate the work of the ministries. These checking functions were also performed by the various state committees under the Council of Ministers.

The distinction between administration, on the one hand, and *kontrol'* (checking on implementation) and coordination, on the other, is fundamental to this analysis of the Stalinist system. It was only the ministries that had the formal authority to give orders to factories, farms, schools, regiments and other institutions. They were the leadership's basic link with the political, economic and social life of the country. State committees, party organs and similar bodies could give orders to enterprises and institutions only through the ministries.[15]

Even amongst the ministries there were those whose major function came closer to checking or supervision than to implementation. For example, the Ministry of Finance, although it directly administered the state banks, was primarily concerned with checking on the financial rectitude of institutions under the command of other ministries. In a similar fashion the Ministry of State Control was supposed to ensure that the work of other ministries' enterprises was up to the mark especially in terms of the quality of their end product.

The line (or "branch") ministries that will be discussed in this section are typified by the Ministry of the Armed Forces, that of Medium Machine-Building, and that of Higher Education. Each had a relatively clearly defined policy sphere over which it had operational control. Ministries operated on the principle of *"edinonachalie"*, or one-man management. In other words the minister's decisions were law for all his subordinates and he took sole and undivided responsibility for the work of his ministry. This pattern of vertical subordination and responsibility was replicated at all levels within the ministry and within its subordinate enterprises and institutions.

It was this direct control over the means of production, of armed force, of education and so on that distinguished the branch ministries from all other sections of the Soviet bureaucracy. It also gave them a head start in the battle for influence over the formation and implementation of policy that was waged amongst the various parts of Stalin's bureaucracy.

The continuous struggle amongst different sections of the

bureaucracy was partly the result of this structural pattern. The existence of parallel bureaucracies – branch ministries to implement and other agencies to check on them – led to an overlapping of responsibilities. Whilst the dividing line between administration and *kontrol'* (checking) may be clear in theory, it is seldom clear in practice. The theory of one-man management was contradicted by the practice of a number of different state, party, Soviet and trade union officials all being held responsible for the work of the same institution. In spite of attempts to meddle in its affairs it was often the ministry that held the whip hand in the resulting struggle for power and influence, partly because they had executive control over institutions and enterprises "on the ground".

Parallelism and overlapping responsibilities will be discussed in later sections of this chapter. It is sufficient here to note that it occurred not only between the state and party hierarchies but also within the Council of Ministers and even inside ministries themselves.

The internal structure of most branch ministries mirrored that of the Council of Ministers itself. Each ministry was divided into chief administrations, or "*glavki*". Some *glavki* were responsible for the day-to-day running of enterprises or institutions. Others were more concerned with particular aspects of the work of all the ministries' subordinate bodies. For example, the Ministry of Ferrous Metals in 1947 had 13 branch-territorial *glavki* administering iron and steel works and 12 "functional" *glavki* in charge of, for example, personnel and pay, production supplies and transport.[16] Besides branch-territorial *glavki* those ministries which controlled a large number of institutions tended to have divisions at union republic level. The Ministry of Light Industry for example had under it similar ministries for the Ukraine, for Georgia and for the other 14 republics that constituted the USSR. The functional *glavki* were complemented by various bodies whose purpose was to advise the ministerial hierarchy, rather as the state committees advised the Council of Ministers. In the Ministry of Ferrous Metals the minister was advised by a Collegium, a "Production *aktiv*" (the activists) and a Technical Council.[17] Within the ministries as outside them, this parallelism and the resultant overlapping of responsibility for each enterprise led to quarrels between *glavki*, collegia and so on. In these struggles those who were in charge of the day-to-day administration of institutions had an important advantage in their access to bargaining resources.

The reasons for the bargaining power of branch ministries and their branch-territorial *glavki* lay in both their formal powers and their actual behaviour. According to article 72 of the Stalin Constitution of 1936 "The ministries of the USSR direct (*rukovodyat'*) the branches of state administration entrusted to them." Article 73 detailed the ministries' responsibility for carrying out decrees of the Council of Ministers and issuing detailed directions on the basis of them. In this latter function lay a significant part of the ministries' power. On the pretext of "filling in the details" of the general directives of their masters they could switch resources from one project or enterprise to another and to "reinterpret" those decisions. Legal limits were set to the extent of these reallocations,[18] but, as will be argued, the checking bodies often lacked the resources and the will to ensure that those limits were not breached.

One of the major advantages the branch ministries enjoyed over their bureaucratic rivals was in terms of sheer size. Of the 57 ministries operating in March 1947, 52 can be regarded as branch ministries. Only five (those of internal affairs, state security, justice, finance and state control) had extensive checking functions.[19] Within the ministerial framework the administrators outnumbered their controllers. Even if one extends one's view into the rest of the Council of Ministers and further into the party bureaucracy, one can see that the checkers were heavily outnumbered by the implementors. By this time the branch ministries must have been employing millions of officials. In contrast the party could muster only 200 000 full-time staff. Each checker had to keep his eyes on a number of implementors. Even if all checking agencies acted in concert (which they did not), the administrators in the branch ministries had important advantages over them in terms of time, specialist training and detailed knowledge.

The specialism of ministerial officials often enabled them to evade the checking activities of their supposed controllers. The relatively narrow field of specialism of each ministry is illustrated by their numbers. Nearly half of the branch ministries were concerned with industry. The area covered by a single people's commissariat for heavy industry before the war was divided up amongst no less than 19 ministries by 1947. There were six ministries in the machine-building sector of Soviet industry alone.

This specialism of ministries is also reflected in the technical training and experience of their staff. Compared to their counterparts of the 1930s the officials of Stalin's branch ministries were much better trained and had far more experience of work in their ministries.

The ministers of the late 1940s had generally received a higher education in the previous decade, in most cases in a field related to the specialism of their ministry. Of a group of seven industrial ministers[20] in 1950 all had a higher education (albeit unfinished in one case); all had at least 15 years' experience of the production branch they were managing in February 1950. All had come to their then ministerial position from a post within this or a similar ministry (four had been deputy ministers in the same ministry).

During the war the power of the branch ministries had been enhanced by the fact that most of their senior officials remained at their desks as the work of their commissariats was often vital to the war effort. In contrast many of the party and police officials who were supposed to check on them were drafted into the forces. The war thus strengthened the hand of the branch ministries in spite of attempts to undermine it after 1945 by reorganising them.[21]

In terms of experience of the work of their agencies the ministerial generation of the 1940s were much better qualified than their predecessors of the previous decade. The 22 industrial ministers in office in 1950 had on average held these posts for more than four years. Their non-industrial colleagues had on average held their posts for three years or more by this time. Many of these had held similar positions throughout the war years. (Their ministries had simply been renamed to cover civilian rather than military production after the war.[22]) Such experienced and highly trained administrators could often evade the control of the more amateur checkers.

The degree of tenure enjoyed by ministerial officials in Stalin's last decade suggests that the checkers (notably party and police officials) did not exercise much control over them. Further their experience of their own ministries allowed branch officials to build up contracts inside and outside their ministries to facilitate their evasion of central directives. For example, A.A. Ishkov as Minister of the Fishing Industry throughout the 1940s (and an employee of the ministry for ten years before that) must have become accustomed to working in certain ways with other administrators and even checkers, ways that were often not in accord with formal rules and orders from the Council of Ministers. This minister in fact survived through the Khrushchev era and was dismissed only in 1980 when he seems to have been part of a multi-million pound swindle. This is an extreme example of not obeying orders. Many more mundane ones will be cited in the following chapters.

Besides their function of implementing general Politburo directives the branch ministries had in practice another important task, the provision of information and advice. This function they shared with most other agencies in the Soviet political system. Just as the various state bodies competed with party, Soviet and other parallel organs for influence over the implementation process, so they also competed for influence over the provision of information and advice that could crucially affect the decisions that they were asked to implement. For example in the process of drawing up the annual and five-year plan directives for the Soviet economy the Politburo relied heavily on information provided by branch ministries. It was these bodies and the agencies, which were supposed to check on them, that could tell the Politburo (via the state planning committee, Gosplan, and the Council of Ministers) how much more a factory or production branch could produce over the next planning period. If plan directives were to be at all realistic they had to take account of such information. That information could be presented in very different ways so as to suggest very different decisions by the leadership. For example the Ministry of Coal might assess its potential for expanding the output of its mines at 5 per cent over the next year, on the basis that 5 per cent was easier for them to achieve than 10 per cent. The checking agencies (like the heavy-industry department of the party's Secretariat) and the leadership might take a more optimistic view, perhaps because they would not have to carry out the directives and achieve the 10 per cent target.

Different sections of the bureaucracy might therefore provide different types of information and advice. In choosing between the various different sources of advice the leadership had to bear in mind the greater specialism and expertise of the branch ministries as well as their final responsibility for implementing the decisions. An example of the relative influence of implementing and checking agencies at this time can be found in the army. The armed forces were directly under the control of the Ministry of

Defence.[23] The ministry and its commanders in the field were supervised or checked upon by a network of political officials ("*zampolity*") under a directorate of the party's Central Committee Secretariat. This system, however, did not involve as much party *kontrol'* as the old Political Commissar system that had been abolished during the war. Throughout the post-war Stalin years, however, the political officers were pressing for a revival of the old system under the Institute of Political Commissars. The fact that this system was not reintroduced owes much to the influence and advice of the ordinary commanders who resented the interference of political officers.[24] These commanders made their views felt partly through the Defence Ministry and its daily newspaper *Red Star*.

In this section a picture has been painted of the various parts of the Stalinist administrative structure vying with each other for influence over the formation and implementation of the leadership's decisions. This competition was the product of parallelism in structure and overlapping of responsibilities both within and outside the ministerial framework. In this struggle for power the branch or line officials had important advantages over their rivals whose main function was to check on the ministries and their officials. These advantages were those of specialism (in both training and experience), of time, and of numbers. In addition they were given certain formal powers over the institutions they controlled (under the system of one-man management) that checking officials did not always possess.

Of course some checking officials especially in the party and the police had advantages of their own in this power game, most notably powers of appointment and dismissal. The extent to which they exercised these powers will be discussed in succeeding sections. However it must be mentioned here that the relationship between implementor and checker was not always one of rivalry and competition. Officials from different administrative hierarchies often found it more productive to cooperate rather than conflict with each other. So-called "family circles" (*krygovaya poruka*) grew up in various regions and policy spheres within which, for example, ministerial, party and police officials got together to decide how to implement policy and what advice and information to give their respective superiors.

When different parts of the bureaucracy competed with each other the leadership could perhaps maintain some control over them on a divide-and-rule basis. When they cooperated the leadership had no way of finding out about or breaking into the family circle. Its control over its own officials could be severely compromised by such behaviour.

THE CHECKING OFFICIALS

The bureaucrats charged with *kontrol'* over the activities of the branch ministries can be divided into three categories, those within the Council of Ministers (including the police), those in the Communist Party, and those in the less important hierarchies like the Soviets and the trade unions. The function of these bodies were, however, not simply to check on the ministries. They were mostly also expected to provide advice and information, to coordinate the work of officials in different regions and branches and in many cases to implement the leadership's policy in some particular sphere. This latter point is best illustrated by the party apparatus' responsibility for certain matters of ideology and that of Soviets for some forms of housing. However their primary function was that of checking, which function was often impossible to distinguish from coordination or advising. If a party secretary found "certain shortcomings" in the work of a ministry in his area it was often as a result of the complaints of other agencies (the secretary performing his coordination function) and could only be put right by providing advice to the ministry or to its superiors.

Checking agencies within the Council of Ministers

The checking bodies within the Council of Ministers can be further subdivided into non-branch ministries and state committees. Of the ministries whose primary function was *kontrol'* rather than implementation, the most feared by far in pre-war Russia were those in charge of the police. The old People's Commissariat of Internal Affairs (the NKVD) had been Stalin's main instrument in his purges of the late 1930s. The NKVD had acquired the power to arrest and imprison or execute anyone suspected of anti-state activity, in other words of opposing the leadership's wishes. In addition, the police had built up a vast economic empire of their own based on prison camp labour. However, in 1943 part of the NKVD was separated off under the new People's Commissariat of State Security (the NKGB, to become the MGB, Ministry of State Security, in 1946). The NKVD (later MVD, Ministry of Internal Affairs) retained control over the prison camp system, although a proportion of the enterprises under its control was transferred to other branch ministries in the post-war reorganisation of the industrial ministries. Thus the MVD was substantially weaker than its pre-war equivalent and in any case became far more like a branch ministry, as many of its checking functions were ceded to the new MGB, whose task was to uncover anti-Soviet activity at home and abroad. The MGB was in charge of the so-called "special sections" that seemed to exist within Soviet institutions at all levels at this time. Their function was to weed out individuals responsible for disobeying instructions or for other forms of "sabotage".

In addition the power of the NKVD had been on the decline for seven years before 1945. The police had gained enormously in power and prestige during the purges of 1936–38. They had been used to decimate the personnel of all the other administrative hierarchies during the "*Yezhovshchina*". Yet the final act of the *Yezhovshchina* was a purge of the police themselves. Many leading NKVD officials followed Yezhov into, at best, obscurity and, at worst, death. Indeed the 18th Party Congress in 1939 specifically renounced mass purges as "outmoded".[25] Thus weakened before the war, the role of the police further declined during the years of the conflict itself. The Nazi invasion gave Russia a sense of national unity and discipline that no police-led purge could impart. The NKVD's role was less vital in wartime and their operations were correspondingly reduced and many of their cadres transferred to other work.

The logic of this argument, however, is that there should have been an even greater need for police functions after the war. The MGB were certainly involved in the mass shooting of returning POWs in 1945–46 and in the pacification of the new areas in the west of the USSR. Their activities were also evident in purges like the Leningrad Affair of 1948–49 and the Mingrelian Affair of 1951–52. Yet the power of the MGB to dispose of members of rival bureaucratic organisations was very much less in 1945–53 than it had been in 1935–38. One reason for this was the efforts of other factions within the leadership to limit the power of the former head of the secret police, Beria. Beria had lost his post of commissar for internal affairs in January 1946 but had remained in effective control of, and had been supported by, the police apparatus during the war. After it, however, A.A. Kuznetsov was appointed as a Central Committee Secretary responsible for police affairs. He was a supporter of Zhdanov's party revivalist faction who were opposed to Malenkov and Beria who had their power base in the ministerial network. Kuznetsov's appointment was intended to dilute Beria's power base and to promote party control over the police. By 1949 Beria had managed to oust Kuznetsov, who became a victim of the Leningrad Affair. With the death of Zhdanov and the executions of Voznesensky and Kuznetsov, Beria's control over the police was freer from challenge in 1949. Even then he had to withstand attacks on his position in the Mingrelian Affair and the Doctors' Plot of 1952–53. In the former many of Beria's supporters in his native Caucasus were purged. In 1952 one of his rivals was probably behind the arrest of several Kremlin doctors. If the investigations into the Doctors' Plot were to be used as a cover for a purge of Beria and his supporters, it was cut short by Stalin's death. Many see the hand of Stalin behind both of these attempts to limit the police chief's power.[26]

Whatever the factional quarrels involved, these events do show that neither Beria's nor Stalin's control over the police was absolute at this time. More importantly for this book the power of the MGB itself was not as great as many seem to have assumed. The best indicator of the MGB's authority is the number of people arrested and imprisoned or shot. In the early post-war years, according to one Western eye-witness, "arrests and deportations did not become a daily obsession (as they had been in the 1930s). with a large number of Russians".[27] Werth argues that this was no longer true after 1948 because of the worsening international situation and the purges sparked off by the death of Zhdanov.

Even then the impact of purges like the Leningrad Affair and the Mingrelian Affair was limited to officials associated with certain regions. In the 1930s the police were used to attack all other elites and administrative hierarchies in the USSR. In the period 1945–53 their impact was much smaller in scale and more sporadic. Many groups of officials in other hierarchies were in practice fairly immune from police persecution. This is reflected in the rate of turnover amongst leading party and state officials in Stalin's last decade. This is very much lower than in the thirties or during the war and in many cases compares quite favourably with the Khrushchev period! Reference has already been made to the degree of job security enjoyed by branch ministers and their officials. Similarly there were no dismissals from the leadership group of Politburo and Secretariat between 1945 and 1949. Over the following four years only two of its members were arrested. Whilst this might not represent moderation to the western reader it does indicate a significant decline in Soviet secret police activity compared to the 1930s. Of the members of the party's Central Committee who were chosen in 1939 and had survived the war exactly half were reelected in 1952 compared to a survival rate of 22.5 per cent from 1934 to 1939, and 66 per cent from 1952 to 1956 (under the post-Stalinist "collective" leadership). There is no sign of the massive turnover of personnel amongst party and state leaders that one would expect to signify a revival in secret police power. Indeed officials of the MGB were not above cooperating with officials of other ministries rather than checking on them. Such activities may have actually been encouraged from the top, for the police chief Beria was a strong ally of Georgi Malenkov whose power base lay in the industrial ministries. Yet, as we have shown, it was not only these ministries that were relatively immune from police persecution but senior party officials as well, although their security of tenure was often less than their state counterparts.[28]

Amongst the checking ministries the MGB was the only one with the power to threaten personnel changes. The other such ministries had to work through the branch ministries and had very few weapons with which to control them. The Ministry of Finance was fairly typical in this respect. It was supposed to be able to investigate the activities of any branch ministry with a view to ensuring its financial rectitude and viability. However, in practice, most enterprises and institutions ran up huge debts to the banks controlled by the Ministry. Meanwhile the banks (notably Gosbank and Prombank, the Industrial Bank) con-tinued to dole out funds to their corporate clients merely because the branch ministry asked them to do so.[29] In the first place the Ministry lacked sufficient numbers of trained specialists to enable it to check up on all the other ministries. In the second place in those cases where it did investigate and find shortcomings there was relatively little it could do to remedy the situation. The Ministry of Finance could only report misdemeanours to higher authority, it could not take corrective action itself. It could not refuse further credit if most of the banks' clients were equally in the red, particularly as those clients were not operating in a market economy. The sums of money that the Ministry dealt with were largely accounting figures, more of interest to itself than to the branch ministries who were more concerned with real resources like tons of coal produced or numbers of engineering students graduated. If a factory or a college went into debt in the USSR, it would not be closed down as long as it continued to produce the end product. The Finance Ministry was typical of checking ministries in that it lacked both the resources to investigate all of its rival implementors and the "teeth" with which to control them. Even a thorough reorganisation of the Ministry in 1948 failed to bring any lasting improvement. The demoted minister Zverev was replaced by Kosygin (a candidate member of the Politburo). The impact of the ensuing reshuffle is perhaps best illustrated by the fact that Zverev was back in his old ministerial seat by the end of the year and remained there until 1960!

There also existed within the Council of Ministers framework a small number of state committees, commissions and councils dealing with such matters as planning, trade, collective farm affairs, and religion. Their role was intended to be one of coordination and advice. Yet they also performed important checking functions. According to the text in use in Soviet legal faculties in the 1940s Gosplan, the state Planning Commission

> unites the activity of separate department and branch organisations. It directs special attention to scrutiny of the execution of plans of national economy.[30]

These were the main functions of all such bodies. For example the Council on Kolkhoz Affairs established in September 1946 was to advise the Council of Ministers on collective farm affairs and to check that farms were not violating the model charter of 1935. It could make only general recommendations to farms; it was not empowered to issue directives to specific *kolkhozy* (collective farms). The number of state committees (and equivalents) grew steadily over the period 1945–53. In 1946 there were four such bodies; by the time of Stalin's death there were eight. As advisers to the Politburo and Council of Ministers they played an important role in the formulation of economic plans and other policy decisions. As checkers on the implementation of those decisions, however, they generally made little impact. They lacked the regional infrastructure and the representatives at grass-root (enterprise or institution) level to enable them to perform this function. In the last pre-war year of 1940 Gosplan, for example, had only 30–40 officials in each one of the USSR's 20 economic regions. Each of these *"upolnomochennye"* (representatives) had to carry out other important functions besides *kontrol'* and verification. Even if a Gosplan official did have the time or the knowledge to uncover the non-fulfilment of a plan directive, there was little he could do about it beyond reporting the matter to the ministry or to the Council of Ministers. The Soviet press in the 1940s is full of such complaints against ministries which ministers made little attempt to remedy. It is little wonder Gosplan and other state committees were prone to cooperate with rather than check on branch ministries.[31]

The Party

Besides the police it was the Communist Party of the Soviet Union (Bolsheviks) (the CPSU(B)) who were potentially the most effective agency for checking on the ministries. In theory they had both the personnel and the power to perform this role. By 1947 the party had six million members, each of whom was supposed to check on the implementation of decisions in his workplace and his neighbourhood and to encourage his non-party colleagues to do the same. In addition the party had the power to appoint and dismiss all the senior officials in the state and other apparati. Most of these state officials were anyway party members ("cadre" members) and hence subject to party discipline.

Yet the party was at this time rather a weak reed. Perhaps the main reason for its weakness was that, whilst its personnel resources were concentrated on its mass membership, the powers of appointment were in the hands of the full-time apparatus of the party. The apparatus was supposed to control the membership through the party discipline mentioned above. In practice the discipline was often weak and the link between the apparatus and the membership in some cases close to non-existent. Before, during and after the war the mass of the party was not ill-disciplined in the sense of being rebellious but was simply inactive. That meant that the full-time officials of the party lacked the resources to control the activities of the ministries. This lack of control was also due to the fact that the cadre members in the ministries did not prove very amenable to party discipline.

The ranks of the party apparatus had suffered as much as any group in Soviet society during the pre-war purges. As many as four or five new faces would appear in a party secretary's post within the space of a year in 1937–38. Furthermore, whereas during the war the ministries regained much of the prestige and influence that they had lost before it, the party secretaries did not. Many were called up and a number lost their lives during the war. Several secretaries of areas occupied by the Germans helped to organise underground resistance. All this was very disruptive of the party's checking role. The laxer economic and cultural policies of the war years perhaps reflect this disruption. As a part of Zhdanov's post-war "party revival" regional party secretaries did begin to enjoy more security of tenure in peacetime. An average of 15 of the secretaries of the 73 largest regional party organisations in the Russian Republic were transferred or dismissed each year over the period 1946–53.[32] The *obkom* secretary of the forties had much more time to get to know his region and its problems than did his predecessors of the 1930s or of the war years.

The party apparatus alone, without the help of its cadre and rank-and-file members lacked the numbers and expertise effectively to check on the work of the branch ministries. By 1955 the party had about 22 000 full-time officials. It would therefore be reasonable to put the size of the apparatus in the late 1940s at around 200 000, about 3000 of whom worked at All Union or Union Republic Level.[33] The branch ministries in Moscow were probably checked on by no more than 1000 officials in the All Union Central Committee Secretariat. Each one of these officials must have had to cover a wide range of activities. Until 1948 the secretariat was organised along "functional" lines with departments for cadres' work, agitation and propaganda, organisation and instruction, agriculture, schools, police affairs and for the administration of the secretariat itself. The "instructors" of any one department simply could not be specialised enough to cover the work of several branch ministries. Even after the secretariat was reorganised in 1948 more along production branch lines there was still only one department (of less than a hundred staff) dealing with, for example, heavy industry, one with the armed forces and one with planning, trade and finance. Each of these spheres was the responsibility of several ministries. The ministerial implementors outnumbered their party checkers by at least ten to one.

The secretariat's main weapon against disobedient state officials was their power of appointment and dismissal under the system of "*nomenklatura*" (list of offices to be filled). However until 1948 this weapon could only be used directly by the cadres' directorate of the secretariat. Only after 1948 could instructors with a branch specialism threaten ministerial officials with dismissal.

Of course the All Union Secretariat had a network of 200 000 party officials in the regions to help them perform their checking functions. But these regional secretaries and instructors were no more specialised in branch terms than their superiors in Moscow. As Jerry Hough has pointed out, their major function is and was the coordination of the work of enterprises and institutions of different ministries within one region.[34] Party officials spent more time coordinating than checking. The training and education of party secretaries was far more generalist and far less technically specialised than that of ministerial officials and even enterprise directors. In 1947 41.3 per cent of *obkom*, *Kraikom* (area party committee) and Union Republic party secretaries had a completed higher education. Of secretaries at the *raion* (district), town and equivalent level only 12.7 per cent had such qualifications. In contrast most ministerial officials had a technically specialised higher education and probably more than three-quarters of factory managers had received a tertiary education. The role of regional party secretaries was to complement rather than challenge ministries' and their enterprises' administrations. They had neither the resources nor the training to mount such a challenge. This is why relatively few ministerial staff were removed from office by the party apparatus in Stalin's last decade, in spite of a *Pravda* editorial of 1946 calling for better cadres' work in the ministries.[35]

Nevertheless most of those staff were themselves party members at this time. Of the six million or so party members in January 1947 about 900 000 were employed in "organs of state and economic administration and in social organisations".[36] As Communists they were members of a Primary Party Organisation (PPO) either within their ministry or within their enterprise or institution. They were therefore bound by the decisions of the PPO, which in practice meant the decisions of its secretary and buro, which in turn often indicated the decisions of a superior party secretary. Normally PPOs were supposed to check on the administrators within their enterprise. In the case of a ministerial PPO, however, that meant in effect that the ministerial officials who constituted the bulk of the *cadre* (office holding) members of the party were supposed to check on themselves. The absurdity of this position was recognised by an amendment to the Party Rules passed in 1939 (on the recommendation of Zhdanov):

> It is the duty of Party organisations in People's Commissariats, which, *owing to the specific conditions of their work, cannot exercise functions of control* to draw attention to defects in the work of their institution, to note shortcomings in the work of the People's Commissariat and of any of its personnel and to communicate their information and opinions to the Central Committee of the CPSU(B) and to the heads of the People's Commissariat (emphasis added).[37]

This could have been a severe test for the corporate loyalty of ministerial staff. Were they to check on their own colleagues and report their inadequacies to the party secretariat and so solve the problem of the party's lack of personnel? In the vast majority of cases it seems that the ministerial official was more loyal to his full-time employer and colleagues in the state apparatus than to the party which he was obliged to join to further his career. Most cadre members of the party restricted their party activities to formal attendance at party meetings.

Some cadre members were, however, coopted to party committees and buros at various levels. For example, many ministers were members of the All Union Central Committee of the Party. A typical *oblast* (provincial) party buro might contain the managers of one or two large local factories. These "*komitetchiki*" (members of committees) were, however, not necessarily any more party-minded and less "state-minded" than the other cadre members.

They were included on buros and committees to facilitate the party's coordination function rather than its checking role. Indeed some saw their role as one of representing ministerial interests within the party rather than of party interests within the state executive machinery.

In any case these committees and buros did not meet with the frequency demanded by the party statutes. For example, it appears that the All Union Central Committee itself did not meet at all between 1947 and 1952. At regional levels, joint sessions of party and state bodies were often held in spite of condemnations from above.[38] This practice carried on the wartime tradition of the State Defence Committee, the Goks, which directed both party and state machines. Within a region some party officials found it more satisfactory to work with local representatives of the ministries rather than against them by checking on them.

Neither were the rank-and-file members of the CPSU(B) an effective mean at the secretariat's disposal for the performance of its checking functions. The membership were grouped into PPOs at the factory, farm or institution where they worked. As early as the 1920s these PPOs began to decline as active organisations. they were further decimated in the purges of the late 1930s. Party membership fell from $3\frac{1}{2}$ million in 1933 to less than 2 million in 1938. In the aftermath of the purge Zhdanov sought to revive the PPO as an organisation to assist party secretaries in performing their checking role. It was on his suggestion that the 18th Congress of the CPSU(B) in 1939 amended its rules to give PPOs "the right of control over the work of the management of the enterprises" in which they worked.[39] In addition, both before and during the war, party membership expanded rapidly. Yet these measures failed to rejuvenate the mass membership of the party for a variety of reasons mostly evident in the war years.

A pre-war recruitment drive had increased party membership in January 1941 to just under 4 million. Even this, an increase of 60 per cent in three years, was dwarfed by the scale of recruitment during the war. Over the years 1941–45 no less than 5.1 million Soviet citizens were admitted to candidate membership of the CPSU(B) and 3.3 million were promoted from candidate to full membership. The result was a serious dilution of the quality of party members. If the pre-war purges had been designed to weed out unsuitable elements and pave the way for a revitalisation of the mass membership, then the wartime admissions policy must have negated the impact of the purges. In spite of the death of many party members on the battlefield, membership in January 1946 was 5½ million, compared to less than four million five years earlier. Most of these had been admitted during the war and thus lacked experience of party work (especially in civilian institutions). Furthermore they received very little training in the responsibilities and duties of a party member. Very often the reason for a person's elevation to the party or from candidate status to full membership was the fact that he had shown bravery in battle.[40] The political credentials of most new entrants were barely scrutinised. Indeed some of these new admissions had previously been expelled from the party![41]

By the end of the war the party's mass membership was therefore seriously lacking in experience and knowledge of all aspects of party work (which for the PPO meant basically checking and the dissemination of propaganda). It reflected a general wartime policy of viewing the party's role as rather superfluous. This policy was the product of two major aspects of wartime conditions. Firstly the leadership seems to have felt that the parallelism inherent in the party/state structure was a waste of scarce resources in wartime. When all personnel and productive effort had to be concentrated on winning the war, party workers and members were of more use fighting at the front or working their machines than in attending party meetings or sending out reports on the inadequacies of their state counterparts. This was why the political commissar system in the army and the political departments in the agricultural machine tractor stations had been abolished during the war. As a result many PPOs had little more than a paper existence during the war, particularly those in factories and farms or in the front line. The second reason for the superfluousness of the PPO during the war was that its political education function could be far better performed by the presence of Nazi troops on Soviet soil. The invasion of a foreign and brutal regime and its takeover of much of the USSR west of Moscow did far more to unify the Soviet people under Stalin's leadership than any amount of party propaganda could hope to do. Both the PPO's major functions – checking and propaganda – became rather superfluous in wartime conditions. As a result admission to the party became more like a battle honour than a sign of any political role.

It was this state of affairs that Zhdanov's post-war party revival was designed to correct. In peacetime the party's checking and propaganda roles would have a renewed importance. The mass membership would have to be trained to perform these roles. The first step was to ensure that admission to the party was made much more selective. As early as 1944 the Army's main Political Directorate (effectively a Department of the Central Committee Secretariat) had called for the exercise of greater care in the selection and training of party members. This was followed by Central Committee Resolutions of July 1946 and March 1947 that sought to put these aims into practice. In the period from January 1947 to October 1952 only 580 000 newcomers were admitted to the party.[42] PPOs were called upon to train and educate those admitted to the party during the war.

Yet in spite of all the publicity attached to this "revival" it had remarkably little impact on the work of the average PPO. The criticisms that were made of these basic units of the party during the war were echoed throughout the 1940s and for long after Stalin's death. Party secretaries at all levels continued to neglect their duties by failing to hold regular mass meetings and elections.[43] Even at the central level no All Union Party Congress was convened between 1939 and 1952, although the rules called for one every four years. With such an example, who could blame an *abkom* secretary for failing to hold his annual *oblast'* conference or the secretary of a factory PPO for neglecting to hold annual elections?

All too often ordinary members of the party were deprived of some of the channels through which they could participate in party work. Where party meetings were held they were often characterised by apathy and irrelevant theoretical work.[44] Whether or not the post-war member was better trained for party work than his pre-war counterpart, he had a far better chance of remaining within the ranks of the party. Very few party members were purged during Stalin's last decade.[45] The reason for this state of affairs could have been that the ordinary party member was of little relevance to the political process at this time in spite of Zhdanov's attempts to revive it.

Party organisations were really run by their full-time officials with little effective help from either cadre or rank-and-file members. Many party secretaries did not seek such help. They saw their role in terms of assisting with and coordinating the work of the local representatives of the state apparatus, rather than in checking upon them. The party as a whole did not recover from the purges or the war during Stalin's lifetime, whilst the state apparatus that had grown up in the early 1930s continued to expand in terms of power and influence during and after the war.

Other checking agencies

Outside the framework of the Council of Ministers and the Communist Party there also existed other bodies charged with checking functions. Perhaps the most notable of these were the Soviets and the trade unions. Soviets existed in all the regions of the USSR as well as at the national level. The Supreme Soviet in Moscow was in constitutional theory the ultimate decision-maker in Stalin's Russia. In practice, however, it met for only a few days each year and then simply approved the draft laws put to it by its Presidium. The local Soviets were similarly powerless. The Presidium and its equivalent in local Soviets, the executive committee, was usually dominated by the local party hierarchy and carried out its wishes. In many important policy areas, such as large-scale industry, executive committees (*ispolkomy*) and Presidia have no legal right to interfere. Only in spheres like housing and the maintenance of public order did they have any executive authority. Most important matters were dealt with by the Council of Ministers' apparatus.

The checking role of the Soviets was supposed to be carried out by the deputies themselves. Deputies were meant to investigate complaints about the behaviour of ministerial officials that were put to them by their constituents. This function they performed in deputies' groups (rather than in the commissions that sometimes perform this role today). Deputies to local Soviets were to form groups within their places of employment to exercise *kontrol'* over the management.

The efficiency of deputies as checking agents was severely limited by their lack of specialist knowledge and experience and by the lack of time they had to perform this function. They were essentially amateur and very part-time officials. At the same time as being a deputy, a member of a Soviet was also expected to hold down a full-time job.

However deputies did manage to voice some complaint about the work of the ministries in Moscow and their offices in the regions. The official journal of the Supreme Soviet, the daily newspaper *Izvestiya*, carried many articles by or letters from deputies on such themes. Where deputies did discover short-comings in the work of departments they could publicise their findings. Publicity was, however, often rather ineffective. Minis-terial replies to complaints published in *Izvestiya* were typically formalistic, uninformative and misleading. Few ministers trembled at the power of deputies even to the Supreme Soviet. Like many other checking agencies they lacked expert knowledge and investigatory resources (time, personnel and so on); they also lacked the sanctions over ministries that party or police officials had at their disposal.

The role of trade unions was similarly limited. Since 1933 Soviet trade unions had been charged with (amongst other things) *"kontrol'* over the effectuation of laws concerning the protection of labour and safety techniques".[46] In the 1940s, however, they had neither the staff nor the authority to carry out these functions. A trade union official who found something wanting in the work of his factory's management could only report the matter to higher authority. That usually meant to the local party organisation, to the MGB or to the ministry in Moscow. In terms of political power both within enterprises and institutions and at the national level, the Soviets and the unions came a poor fourth to the *"troika"* (3-man committee) of ministerial, party and police officials.

CONCLUSIONS: PARALLEL HIERARCHIES AND OVERLAPPING RESPONSIBILITIES

In this chapter we have tried to show that the politics of Stalin's last decade cannot simply be explained in terms of the dictator's character and wishes. Neither can everything be explained by examining his immediate entourage, the Politburo. The reasons are the same in both cases. Just as Stalin depended on his Politburo colleagues for information, advice and implementation, so they in turn depended on the cooperation of their subordinate ministries and party organisations for the same things. Without the compliance and goodwill of those below them Stalin and the Politburo were blind, ignorant and impotent.

Such cooperation could be secured by force, fraud or consent by intimidating, socialising or agreeing with the bureaucracy. It has been suggested here that force was not the main technique used by the Soviet leaders to keep their subordinates in check in the immediate post-war years, although some officials were certainly removed from office and suffered worse punishment. The other two ways of securing bureaucratic obedience were either to convince them that the leadership's decisions were to be carried out come what may or to buy their compliance by making decisions that the bureaucrats agreed with. The fourth alternative was that the bureaucrats did not obey their masters, that they enjoyed some *de facto* freedom to influence Politburo decisions and, if necessary, not to implement them correctly.

How Stalin's officials actually behaved during his last decade can only be assessed by examining the formation and implementation of policy in particular spheres in some detail. Analyses of the Soviet policy-making process, as well as official Soviet accounts of it, often portray the process as a battle between implementors and checkers, with the latter being the more loyal to the Politburo. The major implementors, the government ministries, and the main checkers, the party apparatus, both provided the leadership with information and advice. It is often assumed that it was the checkers' advice that was more readily listened to and that it was the party apparatus that dominated the formation and the implementation of public policy. The preliminary investigations of this chapter suggest that such a conclusion underestimates the impact of the knowledge, experience and sheer numbers of ministerial officials, as well as their direct executive authority. In other words, in the struggle between checkers and implementors over the formation and implementation of Politburo decisions the ministries had more bargaining counters than is often assumed. When this is added to the decline of the party over the pre-war and war years and the failure effectively to revive it thereafter, the stage is set to argue that it may have been the ministerial implementors rather than the party checkers who had greater influence over the end results from leadership decisions.

However it may not be correct to assume that implementors and checkers were always competing with each other for influence. In many cases the Soviet authorities themselves condemned lower level officials for cooperating rather than competing. If implementor and checker decided to cooperate and supply the same information to their ultimate superiors, the latter had no easy way of finding out the truth by playing off party against state officials. If a local party secretary and, for example, the head of a coal-mining trust in his area informed their respective superiors in Moscow that the trust was fulfilling its obligations to improve the quality of its output, then Moscow had no routine method of checking on them. Only in individual cases could it send an inspector from the capital or alert the local police apparatus. There simply were not enough personnel to weed out these "family circles" of checkers and implementors, let alone to bring them to justice. The flow of information to the Politburo may not be accurately represented in many cases by Figure 2.1, which ignores lateral flows of information below Politburo level.

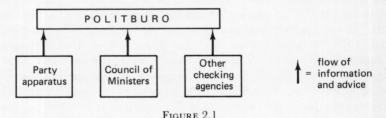

FIGURE 2.1

In some cases at least the situation may better be represented by

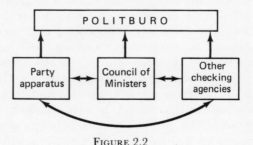

FIGURE 2.2

The reasons for such a pattern of influence lie in the parallelism of the bureaucratic structures involved and in their formal and informal powers and functions.

The fact that the checking institutions were generally organised along lines parallel to those of the ministries meant that the interest of checkers and implementors often coincided. If the political issue were, for example, a matter of distribution of resources between the coal and the oil industries then one would expect the head of a coal trust to find more in common with the party secretary of a coal-producing region or an official in the coal sector of the party central committee's heavy industry department, than with his structural bedfellow, the head of an oil combine. In so far as party and police authorities ran parallel in structure to the ministries they often had more interest in cooperating with them than in checking on them. Where structures were not parallel, as for example, in the case of the regional organisations of the party and police, the checkers normally lacked the specialised knowledge to perform their function. A party secretary of an area with coal mines probably lacked sufficient technical staff effectively to check on local ministerial officials. The resources and power of the ministries that we have already noted may have been enough to persuade other agencies that it was wiser to cooperate with them. Indeed it was one of the prime functions of the party secretary to assist rather than check on the ministries and their enterprises. He was intended to *coordinate* the efforts of various enterprises in his region. That in practice tended to involve procuring and distributing goods for local firms and institutions rather than sending critical reports on them to Moscow. No wonder one *obkom* secretary accused his heavy industry department of being little more than a "despatcher's office" for local enterprises of the ministries in the capital.[47]

The rest of this book will analyse the formation and implementation of policies in industry, agriculture, foreign affairs and culture matters. Throughout these chapters the emphasis will be on determining how far the ministries and the checking agencies tried to influence and succeeded in influencing policies and to what extent they did this in concert or in competition with one another. As will become apparent such an approach opens up a wealth of political debate and infighting below leadership level. The relative impact of this conflict and that which took place within the confines of the Politburo will be assessed in the final chapter.

3　Industrial Policy

INTRODUCTION: THE BACKGROUND TO POST-WAR POLICY ISSUES

The Communist leadership that came to power in Russia in 1917 was totally committed to the idea of industrialising the country. Their ideology was based on the political and economic domination of the industrial working class and for that reason alone the Bolsheviks would have placed industrialisation at the heart of their programme. Lenin and his followers also saw rapid industrialisation as essential to enable them to defend Russia and thus the revolution against foreign aggression and to produce sufficient goods to satisfy all the demands of ill-fed and poorly clothed Russian citizens. After Lenin's demise the "industrialisation" debates of the 1920s amongst Trotsky, Bukharin, Stalin and their followers, which created so much dissension within the Bolshevik Party, were not concerned with whether Russia *should* be industrialised, but only with *how* this could best be achieved. The keynote of Stalin's policies of the 1930s was the need for rapid industrialisation almost regardless of what it cost Russia in human and political terms.

By 1940, under Stalin's leadership, Russia had established her own heavy industrial base. The output of Soviet industry had multiplied nearly seven times over the previous 12 years. However some sectors and regions had grown much faster than others. Emphasising the need for rapid results, the Politburo concentrated on the development of old-established industrial centres and on the basic sectors of heavy industry. Between them the old industrial regions of the Ukraine, and the North West and central economic regions of the Russian Republic (centred around Leningrad and Moscow, respectively) accounted for two-thirds of Soviet industrial output on the eve of the war in 1940. The centrepiece of Stalin's industrialisation policies was the emphasis on the development of heavy industry, and especially on its more traditional sectors. Whilst the heavy industrial "A" sector expanded its output tenfold over the period 1928–40, the output of the consumer goods "B" sector multiplied by only four times. Furthermore the leadership and their planners directed resources more towards traditional branches of industry like coal-mining, iron and steel, and machine building rather than more modern sectors such as oil, chemicals and non-ferrous metallurgy.

The first decade of Soviet industrialisation was also marked by extreme administrative centralisation and by an overwhelming concern for increasing total output with little regard for cost effectiveness or quality of the end product. The Politburo and its ministerial servants in Moscow called on its managers in the provinces to produce more and promised dire consequences if they failed to do so. However, under this system of so-called centralised planning, it was really only quantitative output in which the politicians were interested. Managers therefore tended to raise output by employing more workers rather than by raising labour productivity or installing more modern machinery.

Having established such a pattern for Soviet industrialisation in the 1930s, Stalin and his Politburo were forced radically to revise their priorities by the events of the Great Patriotic War. The major issues of post-war economic policy grew as much from the experience of industry in wartime as from the pre-war industrialisation of the USSR. The rapid German invasion and occupation of old industrial centres in the West in 1941 forced the leadership (in the form of the GOKO, State Committee for Defence) to concentrate resources on building up industry in the less-developed Volga, Urals and Siberian economic regions in the East. Stalin also had to command an even greater concentration on heavy industry than before the war to mobilise and equip a multi-million strong army, navy and air force. To ensure that these priorities were secured the USSR's leadership established an extremely centralised form of administration of some sectors of industry. Directors of major defence industry plants were obliged to report weekly or monthly directly to the political leadership rather than through a variety of ministerial and party levels. In terms of administration and sectoral balance, therefore, Stalin's wartime policies reinforced the general pattern of the 1930s, whilst in regional location policy he significantly altered that pattern. The post-war dilemmas facing the Soviet leaders and their advisors were whether to continue the wartime pattern, or to revert to the industrial proportions of the 1930s or to establish a completely new set of priorities more in tune with the USSR's post-war situation.

The post-war Politburo based their consideration of policy priorities in 1945 partly on their assessment of whether the reasons for the wartime policies were still operative in 1945. Their reason for moving Russian industry eastwards in the war was the Nazi occupation of the Ukraine and many of the industrial areas around Leningrad. German troops advanced as far as the heart of the central industrial region around Moscow in 1941 but were held at the capital city by the Red Army and were soon turning their attention southwards to Stalingrad. With the North Western and Ukrainian regions occupied or isolated from the rest of Russia (as was the oil-producing Caucasus) the Soviet army had to rely on industry east of Moscow to supply its needs. It was to achieve this that industrial plant was evacuated from the west and north-west to the Volga, Urals, Siberia and Central Asian regions in the first year of the war. However, the extent of the evacuation was limited by the speed of the Nazi advance and the immobility of much of the machinery involved. It simply was not possible to evacuate coal mines or shipyards.

Much more important for the growth of the eastern areas was the new investment poured into these regions by the Soviet regime during the years 1941–43.[1] Entire new industries were established in the east and mineral deposits exploited there on a scale never dreamt of before the war. It was, for example, during this period that the Volga–Urals oilfields first came to prominence and that the Karaganda coal basin in the Central Asian republic of Kazaklustan became a major producer.

The effect of the policies of the Goko in the first two years of war was therefore to speed up the industrial growth of the east of the USSR and to bring that of the western areas to a virtual standstill. In contrast the latter years of the conflict saw a slowing down in the east's growth rate and extensive reconstruction of war-damaged areas in the west. As the Red Army began to liberate the occupied areas in 1943 and 1944 so Stalin's leadership began to divert resources away from the east to rebuild the shattered industries of the west. These regions had suffered from the ravages of both armies, as the invader moved east and was then forced back again across the frontier. The retreating Russians had also tried to sabotage mines and factories in 1941 to prevent the Nazis exploiting them. The Germans pursued similar "scorched earth" policies during their retreat two years later. The official Soviet estimates of the loss to her economy ran to 679 billion rubles and up to 20 million dead. Most of the material losses were in the occupied areas of the west; two-thirds of the national property of these regions was destroyed.[2]

The industrial reconstruction of these areas began almost as soon as the occupying armies had been pushed out of a region. The reconstruction of the Moscow coal basin, for example, began as early as 1942. Large-scale reconstruction began further west in mid-1943. To pay for this reconstruction investments in industry east of Moscow were cut back during the last two years of the war. The history of Soviet industrial growth during the war was not solely one of movement to the east. By the end of the war at least one-third of the industrial capital of the "liberated areas" had been reconstructed. The net impact of the Goko's decisions was to increase the proportion of Soviet industrial output produced east of the Moscow-based central economic region[3] from 18.4 per cent in 1940 to 43.2 per cent in 1945. Most of this growth was concentrated in the Urals economic region, with TransVolga and West Siberian industry also growing rapidly. The share of the western liberated areas fell from 33 per cent to 10.8 per cent over the same period. The industrial outputs of the Ukrainian and Belorussian republics in 1945 were only one-fifth and one-quarter, respectively, of their pre-war levels.

Over the war period Soviet industrial output as a whole initially fell dramatically but recovered from 1942 onwards. In 1945 it was 92 per cent of its pre-war level but its regional distribution had changed dramatically. The issue facing Soviet policy-makers in 1945 was whether to continue the wartime distribution policy (which was also that announced by the Party in 1939) or whether to revert to the more westerly locations of the 1930s or to seek some compromise between these two positions. The nature of pre-war and wartime industrial policies determined the issues that were debated amongst Stalin's officials and colleagues during the last decade of his rule.

The rebuilding of the Soviet national economy after the war became known as the reconstruction process. The other central problem, and arguably the more important one, of this rebuilding was the issue of sectoral priorities, particularly the balance between heavy and light industry. Heavy industry denotes the sectors producing means of production rather than of consumption; in other words, producing items for use in factories rather than for consumption by the populace. This "A" sector of Soviet industry includes the defence and armaments sectors. It was, not surprisingly, "A" sector industries that were favoured by Goko during the war at the expense of the light industrial "B" sector producing mass-consumption goods and foodstuffs. Heavy industry had also been the main focus of the pre-war industrialisation drive in the USSR. In 1928, at the start of the first five year plan, the "A" sector accounted for 39.5 per cent of Soviet industrial output; by 1940 it produced 61.2 per cent of that total. At the height of the war it took 84.4 per cent of Soviet output. By 1945 heavy industry was still producing three times as much as light industry. In 1941 and 1942 resources had to be concentrated on producing for the war effort and levels of mass consumption for the civilian population were cut down to subsistence standards or even below. The issue for post-war policy-makers was not simply that of whether to continue the extremes of consumer deprivation experienced by the Soviet consumer in wartime or to revert to the relative hardship of the pre-war era. There were also advocates of a third course, that of reducing the level of "A" sector dominance to substantially below its pre-war level. In other words it was argued that the post-war years might be the time to move the emphasis of Soviet industrial growth more in favour of the consumer.

There was a further issue in post-war sectoral policy connected with the development of the "new" technologically more advanced industries like chemicals and non-ferrous metal products. This was another part of the general reconstruction problem of whether to continue wartime proportions, to revert to those of the pre-war decade, or move towards completely new sets of priorities. The needs of the army for ever more sophisticated weaponry during the conflict and the supply of some advanced western products under the lend-lease scheme both prompted the leadership to stimulate the technological development of Soviet industry in general and new branches in particular. As much of the defence industry had to be reconverted to meet civilian demand in 1945–46 how far could and should the technological advances of the war be continued and built upon in the post-war development of civilian heavy (and indeed light) industry?

The question of technical progress involved the perennial question for the Soviet leaders of how far the USSR should make use of imported goods and technology. During the reconstruction period this concerned Russia's economic relations with her wartime allies in the West and with the defeated nations of Central and Eastern Europe and Asia. In practice "defeated" nations came to include not only those beaten by Russia and her allies in the war (such as Romania as well as the more obvious Germany and Japan), but also those defeated by the Germans themselves in 1938–40 and now under the control of the Red Army. Countries in both these categories, for example East Germany and Czechoslovakia, were in many ways industrially more advanced than the USSR itself. What Stalin's Politburo had to decide in 1945 were, firstly, the extent to which the USSR could make use of the industrial riches of areas as far apart as Dresden and Manchuria to reconstruct and develop their own industry, and, secondly, whether they should help to rebuild the shattered economies of the other nations of Eastern Europe and China. To a large extent these were problems of foreign policy, but those involved in post-war economic policy-making were also closely involved in them.

The other main area of industrial policy dispute amongst Soviet politicians in the reconstruction period was that of administrative method. During the war (and to some extent before it) industrial policy had been made and implemented under very close scrutiny from Moscow, at least in key armaments and heavy industry sectors. Two factors made such a high degree of centralisation less feasible after the war. One was the quantity of human and other resources needed to police such a system, especially in peacetime when people's compliance with Moscow's orders could not so easily be relied upon. In wartime patriotism and common fear of the invader brought the lower official closer to his superiors in Moscow than was possible in peacetime. In 1945–46 the Politburo had to decide whether a high degree of centralised control could be achieved either through the use of force (as in the industrialisation drive of the early 1930s) or through a massive propaganda exercise (like the "Stakhanovite" and "socialist competition" campaigns of the mid 1930s and the immediate pre-war years). The alternative, advocated by some politicians and planners, was to allow much more decentralisation, permitting ministerial officials and factory directors greater freedom to make their own decisions (albeit within broad parameters set in Moscow). This necessarily involved the introduction of some disguised market mechanism, using prices and profit levels as levers to control industry from the centre. It may come as something of a surprise to many Westerners that such methods were advocated and even introduced to a limited extent in the Stalin era.

Issues like decentralisation and the development of new technology came more to the forefront of political discussion from about 1948–49 when the reconversion and reconstruction of Soviet industry were basically complete. During the first two or three post-war years far more attention was paid to producing as much as possible, almost regardless of the cost and quality. The obvious need to rebuild rapidly led to an acceptance of these methods by most politicians, managers and other advisors. The debates of 1945–47 were thus more concerned with basic priorities of sectoral and regional policy. As in the first five year plan period (1927–32) the philosophy of production at all costs seemed to work. After a slump in industrial output in 1946 (as factories were reconverted from arms production to civilian output) pre-war aggregate output levels were regained in 1947; by 1950 the output of Soviet industry was running at a staggering 73 per cent above its pre-war level. Even allowing for the exaggerations of official Soviet statistics[4] this was a tremendous achievement. However, there were signs that the rate of growth was beginning to slow down and that, especially from a technological and an administrative point of view, Soviet industry was beginning to fall into a straitjacket comparable with that it experienced in the late 1930s. Although decentralisation and development of newer branches of industry was advocated in Stalin's last decade very little was done until after the leader's death. It was Khrushchev in the mid-1950s who pushed through reforms aimed at decentralising Russian industry and building up its neglected modern branches like chemicals and computers.

The Goko's wartime policies thus affected Soviet industry in many ways and in some of them deflected it from the path planned in the 1930s. The first option open to post-war policy-makers was broadly to continue wartime policies but this was often not feasible. For example the wartime policy of producing as many guns and as little butter as possible could not be continued (at least to the same extent) in peacetime. Equally the second alternative of reverting to a 1930s pattern of industrial policies was not always very inviting and in some cases would have been rather stupid. For example, no one seriously advocated that the production of the eastern industrial regions should be cut back to its 1940 levels after the war. That would have involved closing down perfectly efficient factories and transferring their equipment thousands of miles to the west at enormous cost. The war and the demands it made on Soviet industry gave in its aftermath a golden opportunity to rethink industrial policy and to revamp the Stalinist Command Economy of the 1930s. Even the defeated nations like Germany and Japan made good use of the reconstruction period to build the bases for two of the strongest economies in the world today. The possibilities open to the victors in 1945 should have been even greater than those available to their defeated opponents.

THE FORMATION AND IMPLEMENTATION OF INDUSTRIAL POLICY, 1945–53

The first major statement of post-war economic policy was to come with the Fourth Five Year Plan. It was announced that preparations for it had begun in September 1945 and that it would be presented to the USSR Supreme Soviet for its (formal) approval early in 1946. In fact the plan, which was to cover the years 1946–50, had been the subject of debate and preparation long before the end of the war. As early as mid-1943 it was reasonably clear to the Soviet leaderhip and their advisers what their main policy problems would be in the post-war context.

Regional priorities

Regional policy had been very much a live issue before the war. The 18th Party Congress of 1939 had called for the development of "hotbeds" of industrial growth in the east of the USSR, as well as the establishment there of armaments factories that would act as duplicates for those in the west in the event of an invasion. The aim of developing the east was to exploit the rich raw material resources of the Volga, Urals and Siberian regions and to lessen Soviet dependence on the industrial areas of the west that were so vulnerable to an invasion. The same congress in approving the Third Five-Year Plan also called for the complex development of each of Russia's economic regions. "Complex development" meant building up basic industries like fuels, metals and machine building in each region. The rationale behind complex development was, firstly, to lessen the strain on the USSR's overloaded transport system. This system relied heavily on a railway network that could not cope with any further substantial increases in inter-regional freight traffic. The advocates of complex development wanted not only to reduce the need for such inter-area shipments but also to develop industrially the more backward ares of the USSR, particularly those inhabited by the minority nationalities. By developing areas like the Central Asian republics the Soviet regime felt that it could "buy" the loyalty of these peoples who had been forced to join first the Russian empire and later the Soviet state.

The decisions of 1939 thus reflected the views of those who wanted to see the faster development of the eastern rather than the western regions. The developments of the war must have pleased these advocates. However, that was not to say that by 1945 no-one was arguing for the further development of the east. As we shall see again and again in this chapter, merely because the leadership had decided on a policy, incorporated it in a five year plan and carried it out during the war, this did not guarantee the continuation of that policy thereafter. The proponents of more industrial development in the west had a powerful new argument in 1945, that of the need to reconstruct the liberated areas. They were in no mood to allow the decisions of 1939 to be simply repeated in 1946.

Debates over the nature of the regional policy in the first post-war plan took place within the leadership, amongst its academic and staff advisers, and amongst lower party and state officials with narrower departmental interests. These debates were not only permitted to take place, they were conducted partly in public in the pages of journals and at meetings. The leadership's policies were influenced by these discussions and arguments.

That the Politburo were divided on regional priorities is not very surprising. Stalin's Politburo was composed of people with specific departmental or regional responsibilities and thus interests. There is every sign that they were encouraged to air their different interests and opinions within the confines of the Politburo provided that they made no obvious attempt to challenge Stalin's ultimate authority. They even hinted at their differences in public, using the "language of conflict" in vogue at the time. For example, a number of prominent politicians made allusions to their views on regional policy in their speeches before their (uncontested) elections to the Supreme Soviet in February 1946. Voznesenskii, the head of Gosplan, in his speech made great play of the industrial potential of the liberated areas. He made no criticisms of development in the east. Such obvious conflict was avoided by leading figures in public speeches. He simply ignored the future of the eastern areas altogether in this speech. In contrast his Politburo colleague Zhdanov proclaimed that further development of the east was a key part of the post-war regional policy.[5] Interestingly these two leading figures in what McCagg calls the "Economic Voluntariest" and the allied "Party Revivalist" factions seemed to disagree on the regional issue.

Speaking some months earlier on the 28th anniversary of the Bolshevik Revolution, Molotov had emphasised the need to develop the new western areas of the USSR in the Ukraine and the Baltic States, mainly to ensure their loyalty to the Soviet regime. The party journal *Bolshevik*, which published his speech, conspicuously omitted all reference to this point in its commentary on it.[6] This omission pointed to some disagreement between Molotov and the editors of Bolshevik, men who formed part of the party apparatus controlled by Zhdanov. The editors may well have been covertly reflecting their own views and influencing their superiors. It is possible that Politburo members gave public voice to their views in order to gain support from below the leadership's ranks for their opinions. They were in no sense seeking mass electoral support, for the ordinary Russian would understand nothing of the "language of conflict" they were using. They were seeking to appeal to a relatively small circle of officials and advisers who were, as it were, "in the know". Why else should the members of Stalin's close ruling circle make their views public?

An excellent example of the political links between leaders and officials is provided by the debates within Gosplan in 1945.

Ostensibly these discussions concerned the question of "regionalisation" (*"raionirovanie"*), that is, of how to divide the USSR up into regions for the purposes of economic planning and development.[7] However this problem of where to draw the boundaries between regions raised more fundamental issues in regional policy, particularly that of whether to perpetuate the existing geographic distribution of Soviet industry.

On 5 July 1945 the chairman of the State Planning Agency N.A. Voznesenskii presented the report of an investigatory committee on regionalisation. This report recommended that the USSR be divided into 17 regions each distinguished by its current industrial specialisms, irrespective of administrative boundaries. The reasoning behind this proposal was that each region would continue to concentrate on its existing industrial specialism. The oil industry, for example, would continue to be based on Baku and the Volga oilfields, in spite of the existence of large deposits in Siberia. Such an approach implied a continuation of existing patterns of industrial location (at least after the west of the USSR had been reconstructed). It would therefore have discriminated against the further industrial growth of the less developed areas in the east and south of the USSR.

Another significant implication of this specialisation approach was that economic criteria were accorded more importance in regional policy-making than were political concerns, such as the benefit to the minority nationalities and to the defence sector. The rationale of this regionalisation was not only to perpetuate the locational status quo but also to establish the principle that industrial investments should be concentrated in areas specialising in one type of industry that could promise quicker returns on those investments. Over a limited time period of, for example, five years, a new iron and steel works could be built in the South Ukraine (the ferrous metals centre of the Soviet Union) and could be expected to be in production and to be approaching peak efficiency. A similar works in the underdeveloped areas of East Siberia would take longer to build and it would be many years in achieving its peak of efficiency. Only over ten or fifteen years could the Siberian works hope to yield the same returns on investments as the Ukrainian one, as Siberia lacked the industrial infrastructure, skilled labour and so on that the Ukraine possessed (although Siberia did have rich raw material reserves). Over an even longer period these reserves might enable the Siberian plant to become more productive than the Ukrainian equivalent. The key to the specialisation policy of Voznesenskii's report was that it envisaged a policy of securing maximum economic returns from investments over a relatively short time period. The fact that Voznesenskii's proposed regions often cut across existing administrative boundaries only emphasised disregard of the report's authors for political returns.[8] Concentrating future industrial growth on the developed and specialised areas of the west and centre often meant ignoring the political benefits of investment in the east. In the first place growth in the east would help to buy the loyalty of the various non-Russian nationalities of these areas, notably in the Central Asian republics. Secondly, as the Nazi invasion had proved, there were important defensive advantages in establishing major industrial plants in the east, far distant from any hostile army.

Yet it was not mainly these non-economic arguments that Voznesenskii's opponents within Gosplan used to dispute his regionalisation proposals. The policy favoured by a group headed by A.V. Korobov, head of Gosplan's capital construction department, called for a regionalisation based on the complex development policies of 1939. Far from being specialised in one or two industries each region was to produce its own iron and steel, machinery, fuels, construction materials and so on. The justification for this aim of regional self sufficiency was not mainly in terms of political benefit, although Korobov had mentioned development of the minor nationalities as a spin-off from his proposals. The reasoning behind complex development, for some Gosplan officials at least, was economic. Complex development would yield greater returns on investments in the long run as it would encourage the development of the rich raw material deposits (metal ores, fuels and the like) of the east. It would also reduce the need for inter-regional transport of goods by the seriously over-loaded railway network.

In spite of Voznesenskii's exalted position as a Politburo member, it was the Korobov faction that won the day within Gosplan. Twenty days after Voznesenskii had presented his report a new commission was established to work out a regionalisation based on complex development criteria. The political climate of 1945 allowed discussion of basic issues of industrial policy to an extent that the apparent[9] wishes of a Politburo member could be overruled by his subordinates. However, that discussion had to take place within certain parameters specified in the language of conflict in use at the time. These discussions were kept within a relatively small circle of planners, advisers and politicians. The Gosplan debate was not public knowledge at the time although senior officials and advisers outside Gosplan were allowed to air publicly their views on regional policy, although only in small circulation journals like Gosplan's own _Planovoe Khozyaistvo_ or the Party's _Bol'shevik_.[10]

The regionalisation debate exhibits another clear feature of the language of conflict of the 1940s. Discussions of quite basic issues were allowed and even encouraged provided that they were conducted in technical rather than political terminology. This explains why economists and planners were generally reluctant to bring openly political criteria into their arguments. The future direction of regional policy was obviously a political problem but could be openly discussed as though it were a purely economic one, although the participants were probably well aware of the political arguments and implications.

The other mode of political debate available at the time involved the discussions of particular cases as a covert way of raising more general issues. For example at the April 1945 session of the Supreme Soviet several deputies from the liberated areas called for a greater concentration of resources on their own regions. Whilst not openly criticising the wartime regional policy of eastern development, they did so by implication, by detailing the problems of their own (western) areas.

It was in the light of pressures like these that the regional policy decisions of 1945–47 were made. The first decision, on the new regionalisation project, was made to favour the east but later decisions were much more in the nature of compromises between the specialisation and complex development factions and therefore between the advocates of the west and those of the east. Before analysing those decisions, however, a note of caution must be struck. Merely because a decision had been taken and published as a decree or resolution that did not mean an end to political wrangles. For the decisions still had to be implemented. In the Soviet Union in the post-war decade (arguably today) almost as much political energy had to be expended to ensure that decisions were actually carried out as to influence the nature of the decision in the first place. In the case of the regionalisation the new Commission's report (to be guided by complex development policies) never saw the light of day. As a result of the old regional divisions based mainly on pre-war regional specialisms, continued to be used for planning purposes. In terms of end results, therefore, it was only after Stalin's death that the specialisation approach to regional planning was modified by Khrushchev's establishing of regional economic councils (*"Sovnarkhozy"*).

In regional policy the battle for influence over policy formulation before the new Five Year Plan went in favour of advocates of the Eastern region, especially within some sections of Gosplan and the Party apparatus. This pattern was continued in the Fourth Five Year Plan of April 1946 and in Politburo decisions over the following twelve months, although some concessions were made to those who, like Molotov (and possibly Voznesenskii), wanted to see the west rebuilt.

The new plan could not under the chaotic circumstances of reconstruction and reconversion of industry to civilian needs be anything but a *general* guide to leadership policy priorities. As a detailed step-by-step programme for the ensuing five years it was clearly inadequate. The amount of effort put into its preparation and the propaganda campaign surrounding its official promulgation do show, however, that it was meant to tell the implementors of economic policy what the Politburo wanted their priorities to be.

The new plan reflected the Politburo's decisions to maintain development of the east after the war in several respects. For the first time in such a plan precise and detailed targets for the economy of each Union Republic were published. In presenting the plan to the Supreme Soviet Voznesenskii (in a speech no doubt cleared with his Politburo colleagues in advance) restated the leadership's commitment to complex development. This in turn was reflected in the plan's provisions for the development of certain basic heavy industries in each Union republic and in the decision to reduce inter-regional transport flows, whilst concentrating more resources on railway freight *within* regions.

The western areas were by no means ignored in the plan. Forty-six per cent of investment in Soviet industry was to go to the liberated areas which had accounted for only one-third of Soviet output before the war. In summary the plan decisions sought to develop the east and rebuild the west, something that could only be done at the cost of expansion in the central and northern economic regions and the unoccupied areas in the North West and North Caucasus.[11]

The continued commitment to eastern development by a majority in the leadership (probably led by Zhdanov with Stalin's approval and linked to the "Party Revival") was reflected in decisions rubber-stamped by the Supreme Soviet in 1946 and 1947. Decrees of August 1946 and May 1947 provided substantial material incentives to Soviet citizens willing to work in the east, even for a limited number of years. On the administrative front several ministries (such as those for oil and coal) were divided into eastern and western ministries. In January 1947 Gosplan's regional department was reorganised by the creation within it of a sector for each Union Republic. By these changes the leadership sought to create organisations specifically committed to the complex development of particular regions.

One of the reasons for these reforms was no doubt to overcome the bureaucratic interference that prevented the plan's objectives being fulfilled. Whilst the plan for the overall expansion of Soviet industry from 1946 to 1950 was overfulfilled by 17 per cent the target for many eastern regions was not achieved. For example, whilst national industrial output rose by 88 per cent over the period 1946–50 that of the Urals region actually *fell* by 4 per cent. Neither was the target for the liberated areas quite achieved, the actual expansion of 3.9 times indicating an output level in 1950 of 98 per cent of its plan target.

The main beneficiaries in Soviet industry in the Fourth Five Year Plan period seem to have been the old industrial areas of the north west and centre, including many that had suffered relatively little in wartime. These were precisely the areas that were not supposed to expand so rapidly according to the Plan. Yet this apparent reversal of priorities was never signalled by any change in leadership policy. The fact was the regional policies of 1946–47 were simply not carried out as the leadership had intended.[12] In spite of continued debate on regional policies and related matters amongst Gosplan and party officials, academics, deputies to the Supreme Soviet and so on,[13] the end results were being determined by the detailed operations of the branch ministries, backed by supporters of their interests and of the established industrial areas. The most apt summary of the activities of ministers and managers in diverting resources to the old industrial areas is provided by Korobov, once again using (in June 1947) the Party's journal *Bolshevik*. He wrote:

In the past year . . . many ministries and organisations paid insufficient attention to the business of the development of the eastern regions.[14]

For most of the Five Year Plan period branch ministries and construction ministries concentrated their attention and resources on their established factories around towns like Moscow, Leningrad and Gorki. Most showed very little interest in building up new projects in the more easterly (or western) parts of the USSR. Supplies of scarce labour, raw materials, construction services and transport facilities were concentrated on the old areas rather than the new. It was the various branch ministries that controlled these supplies. The story of areas like Belorussia (in the west) and Siberia (in the east) in the late 1940s is one of construction projects and whole factories lying idle for want of men and materials. Managers of such enterprises complained frequently in the press and at conferences, as did the party and Soviet representatives of their regions. The butt of their criticisms was almost always one of the ministries in Moscow. Either the Ministry of Railways was not sending enough oil-tank wagons to the Urals or Molotov (now Perm) *oblast'* in Siberia was chronically short of bricks.

The reason for the branch ministries' actions is not hard to find. Labour, materials and fuel were all in short supply in the USSR after the war and each ministry had to make the best of what it had to fulfil its overall output target. In order to achieve this aim the ministries concentrated scarce resources on existing firms in developed areas where they would yield much quicker returns than if they were locked up for years on end in some gigantic project in Eastern Siberia.

The very fact that they were mostly branch rather than regional organisations made the ministries keener to expand the output of the branch as a whole in the shorter term rather than pursue longer-term regional objectives.

However, many of the checking organisations, such as the party, the Soviets, and even the police were organised along regional lines. Why did they not force the ministries to act more in accordance with the plan's (and thus the leadership's) regional priorities? Their failure to do so was partly due to their own weaknesses, partly to their lack of incentive to do so and partly to the political wrangles that were continuing in the Kremlin.

The shortcomings of regional party and Soviet organisations have already been analysed in an earlier chapter. They lacked the numbers, the knowledge and the direct operational control to challenge the power of the ministries. Representatives of the Soviets and the party apparatus did frequently voice regional interests against the ministries, but then many of their colleagues had very different points of view. The Soviets and the party were not uniformly against the ministries and in favour of developing the east and the western liberated areas. Deputies and Party Secretaries from the established industrial areas had a clear interest in promoting their areas against their newer rivals and frequently voiced that interest.

Many party, Gosplan, and Supreme Soviet officials at the USSR level also had branch rather than regional responsibilities. The Supreme Soviet Presidium, the All-Union Secretariat of the Party and most sectors of Gosplan were organised (in part) along production-branch rather than regional lines. Until 1948 the Secretariat under Zhdanov was organised along functional lines, which limited the expression of branch or departmental interests. After his death, however, the Secretariat was reorganised along departmental lines with one department checking on (perhaps) three or four ministries. The effect of this reform was to bring secretariat and ministerial interests closer to each other on regional issues.

The restructuring of the Secretariat was no doubt part of the shake up in Kremlin politics which followed Zhdanov's death. He especially amongst the Politburo had espoused the revival of the influence of the party apparatus. Stalin seems to have approved of this revival as a means of counterbalancing the power of the ministries, whose champion was Malenkov, and of Beria's secret police. Zhdanov's death upset this balance of power within the Politburo. In the context of regional policy Zhdanov and many party officials favoured the new industrial regions. After 1948 Malenkov, Beria, the branch ministries and the police came to the fore. Thereafter the complaints of regional party officials and others fell on increasingly deaf ears in the Kremlin.

The only weapons available to regional party officials in their battle with the ministries was to complain to higher authority in the Central Secretariat or the Politburo. Especially after 1948 these bodies were not very responsive to the interests of the less developed regions. Even the party apparatus' famed power of appointment and dismissal through the *nomenklatura* system was of little use in this respect. Senior ministerial officials came on the *nomenklatura* lists of the *branch* departments of the Central Committee Secretariat in Moscow. Officials of branch departments in the party (and in Gosplan's apparatus) had no departmental interest in enforcing the leadership's regional policy.

The changes in the balance of power in the Politburo after Zhdanov's death and the arrest of Voznesenskii in 1949 may have reduced the leadership's commitment to complex development policies, although no public indication of this was ever given. The Fifth Five Year Plan announced in 1952 had little to say about regional policy. The issues of the 1940s really came to a head only after Stalin's death. The Gosplan debate was reopened by Khrushchev in 1954 and the discussion culminated in his *Sovnarkhoz* reform of 1957. From the point of view of the 1940s the most interesting feature of this reorganisation was that it recognised the reasons why some regions had been more neglected than others in Stalin's last decade. Khrushchev set up regional economic councils (*"sovnarkhozy"*) – regionally-based bodies which took over much of the day-to-day running of the economy from the central ministries. However, the ministerial lobby continued to fight back; one of the first acts of the Brezhnev leadership that overthrew Khrushchev in 1964 was to abolish the *sovnarkhozy* and restore the branch ministries to their former position of power.

The success of ministerial opposition to the regional policy of 1945 was partly due to the lower priority accorded to this aspect of economic policy after about 1948. By this time the Soviet economy had been basically restructured along civilian lines and had regained the output levels of 1940. In fact industrial output in 1946 *fell* by one-fifth to 76 per cent of its pre-war level. This was largely due to the civilianisation process, although the poor agricultural performance in that year also had an effect. Thereafter industrial output rose steadily, regaining pre-war levels in most major sectors by 1948. By 1950 industrial output was officially measured at 73 per cent above its 1940 level.

This was a staggering achievement in view of the devastations of wartime and the need to adjust to peacetime conditions. To some extent, however, the Politburo's targets for all industry were achieved by channelling resources into regions and sectors that the leadership had not intended should be given such a priority.

Just as the bureaucracy had directed its efforts particularly at the established industrial areas, so they also gave most attention to the higher growth sectors of the 1930s – the basic extractive, processing and manufacturing branches that form "heavy industry" (in Soviet terms the "A" sector).

Sectoral priorities

The Keynote of Stalin's first three Five Year Plans was the primacy of heavy industry. The needs of agriculture and consumer goods were sacrificed to the building of a vast heavy industrial base. Stalin (and Trotsky for that matter) argued that a backward nation like Russia could only be industrialised by first concentrating on those industries producing the means of production. They wanted to expand consumer goods production only when the heavy industrial base was large enough to provide the machinery and materials for that expansion. Stalin also sought the development of heavy industry to provide for Russia's defence. Most of the major war industries were included in the "A" sector. As a result of these policies the "A" sector formed 61.2 per cent of Soviet industrial output in 1940, and the consumer goods "B" sector only 38.8 per cent. The average Soviet worker's standard of living in that year was little above what it had been fifteen years before, but Russia's heavy industrial and arms bases had been built.

The Goko's wartime priorities showed, as in other combatant nations, a further cutback of consumption to virtual subsistence levels (or below in some areas like besieged Leningrad). In 1942 only 15.6 per cent of industrial output was in the form of consumption goods. As wartime conditions eased so this proportion rose steadily to 25.4 per cent in 1945. Consumption levels were, however, still well below even the non-too-high pre-war standards.

It was not surprising, therefore, that some Stalinist politicians favoured a better deal for the Soviet consumer in 1945. Some argued that the heavy industrial base that had made Russia strong enough to resist the invader was now adequate to fuel the development of consumer goods production. In putting forward such ideas some politicians were clearly aware of the need to buy the political loyalty of the Soviet citizen, especially in the new areas added to the west of the USSR in 1940.

Amongst the post-war planners and politicians, however, there remained a strong industrial lobby. These people saw the first post-war priority as the reconversion of war-industry to meet the needs of civilian heavy industry. To them the "A" sector was still the prime focus of attention in the industrialisation drive. Many economists and politicians became quite emotive on the subject of the primacy of heavy industry. To Korobov of Gosplan, it was this that distinguished the socialist form of economic development from the capitalist.[15]

In the discussions of sectoral policy that preceded the publication of the Fourth Five Year Plan the advocates of heavy industry relied heavily on such "ideological" arguments. They also made much play of the need to keep expanding the "A" sector to provide an adequate base for the defence of the USSR. As post-war tension increased (especially over Greece and Iran)[16] so their arguments acquired more validity.

Light industry also had its defenders in Gosplan and the ministries. The Finance Minister Zverev tells us in his memoirs how he put pressure on the leadership to tell the planners to direct more resources towards the "B" sector.[17] Zverev wanted more consumer goods and foodstuffs on the market to mop up the surplus purchasing power that had accumulated during the war. With little to spend their money on in wartime Soviet consumers had saved it. After the war there were not enough goods to buy and the result was a flourishing black market charging exorbitant prices. The finance ministry wanted to undermine this black market by increasing legal supplies of consumables. It also sought to do so by devaluing people's savings in 1947[18] and by charging higher state prices for goods purchased beyond the amount specified in each citizen's ration (these were called "commercial" prices).

Within the Politburo it seems clear that Zhdanov and Mikoyan were firm advocates of consumerism. Yet not all of the "party revivalist" and "economic voluntarist" factions shared this point of view. Voznesensky for one appeared to lean more towards the heavy industry point of view.[19] Neither were all the "anti-insurrectionists" and pro-ministerial members in favour of heavy industrial development above all else. Molotov, for one, stressed the need to satisfy consumer demands in an official speech in

November 1945.[20] He made the interesting point that many Soviet citizens had travelled abroad during the war and had experienced (to a degree) higher living standards there. Their higher expectations in the post-war era had to be met in part by Soviet industry after 1945. Otherwise (although Molotov did not spell this out) consumer frustration might lead to civil disorder. As a matter of fact nationalist anti-Soviet movements in several areas of the USSR continued to flourish for at least two years after the end of the war. Support for them was partly fuelled by poor supplies of consumer goods and especially of foodstuffs after the drought of 1946.

The line-up in the Politburo on the sectoral issue, therefore, by no means coincided with that over the regional issue. Although, for example, Zhdanov and Malenkov were clearly opponents on most issues, their support amongst their colleagues varied according to the policy area concerned. This explains why one "faction" could never dominate or remove its opponents. No one group was always in a minority.

Much the same could be said of Stalin himself. He did not take sides clearly on the sectoral issue at this stage. His position was partly dictated by the balance of opinion in his leadership (which was in turn affected by opinions amongst their subordinates) and by the course of events themselves. As fear of an invasion from the West increased, so Stalin (and others) moved more towards the heavy industry lobby. In February 1946, however, the wartime East–West alliance still functioned (after a fashion). Stalin, in his last public speech for six years, then announced a series of targets for the development of major industrial sectors over the next two decades. However, he did not favour one side of the sectoral argument. Advocates of both heavy and light industry quoted parts of his speech in support of their arguments![21]

Two months later the plan was published. In presenting it to the Supreme Soviet Voznesensky announced a planned growth rate for the "B" sector of 17 per cent per annum over the next five years. That implied an expansion rate for the consumption industries of almost three times that of heavy industry. Yet, because of wartime contraction, the light industry sector would still be producing only 34 per cent of Soviet industrial output in 1950 compared to 38.8 per cent in 1940. In other words the leadership planned a rapid expansion of the "B" sector, mainly at the expense of the war industries, although heavy industry was to remain at the heart of the national economy.

Over the following nine months, however, it became clear that light industry was not meeting its targets. To some extent this could be attributed to the drought and subsequent poor agricultural performance of 1946. It was also due to familiar patterns of behaviour on the part of All Union ministries. As managers of light industrial plants were trying to convert their enterprises to civilian production they ran into widespread shortages of supplies of raw materials, energy, labour and construction materials. Most of these supplies were controlled by branch ministries, who seemed to favour the heavy industrial sector.

The leadership's response to this was swift and decisively in favour of consumer goods. In November and December 1946 decrees were passed aimed at increasing the output of consumer goods by both small-scale local and cooperative industry and large scale All Union branch ministries. Resources were reallocated away from "A" sector industries to light industry and several Five Year Plan targets for consumables were raised by between 2 and 9 per cent.

Within a year, however, the changing international situation was pressurising the Politburo towards a greater emphasis on the "A" sector. The death of Zhdanov in 1948 and the purge of his allies and supporters exerted a further push in the same direction.

After the rejection of the Marshall Plan by the USSR and her allies in 1947, East–West tension escalated as the countries of Europe found themselves firmly divided into two camps. The Cold War continued through a series of near-open conflicts between the Americans and the Russians, notably the Berlin Blockade and the Korean War. Once again, as in 1940–41, most of the Soviet leadership felt the need to reconcentrate resources on those sectors of heavy industry producing weapons and ammunition for the Armed Forces. Although no formal decision to divert resources away from the production of consumer goods was announced at this time, it may well have been made. Considerations of national security probably prevented its publication.

The worsening of relations between the two superpowers was one reason for the failure of light industry as a whole to reach its plan targets in 1950. The planned output for the "B" sector was only 95 per cent realised; that for the "A" sector was *over*fulfilled by 28 per cent. Yet this inequality of fulfilment was not solely due to the Politburo's apparent change of priorities in 1947–48. It was also due to continued ministerial sabotage.[22]

Resources for building new plant and for keeping existing machinery running at full capacity were all in short supply in post-war Russia. However many ministries in Moscow and their local organs made a point of ensuring that scarce supplies were directed above all to heavy rather than light industry. In the building of new factories the construction ministries and those who supplied to them favoured their "A" sector customers. Light industry was forced to rely far more on its own profits to finance its expansion. Those profits were more heavily taxed than were those of the "A" sector (which was in any case more heavily subsidised). The ministries controlling labour, machinery, energy and other supplies to all sectors of industry were persistently criticised in the Soviet press for unduly favouring heavy industry. Without sufficient inputs light industry could not meet its plan targets.

The central ministries in fact had little interest in supplying "B" sector factories. There was no construction or machine-building ministry specialising in light industry's needs. The officials of these and other ministries tended to favour heavy industry because "A" sector construction projects and factories generally were larger than "B" sector concerns and so were "better customers". In addition heavy industrial firms were more likely to be able to do favours in return for the allocation of scarce supplies. If a construction ministry was (for example) short of bricks or machines it could acquire these by giving priority to heavy industrial customers like the Ministry of Construction Materials or one of the machine-building ministries. This exchanging of favours (or even outright barter) was (and is) common in Soviet industry. Light industrial plants (on average) have fewer scarce materials to offer as bribes to their suppliers, clothing, consumer durables and food being of less use to factories than steel or machinery.

There is also some evidence that many senior ministerial officials were more heavy- and light-industry minded. Most had been trained and gained their experience in the 1930s when priority to heavy industry was so central to the official ideology. Such a "steel eater" mentality was reinforced after the war by many planners and academic advisers. G.P. Kasyachenko, the chief editor of Gosplan's house journal, damned any opposition to the priority of heavy industry "Trotskyite" or "Bukharinite".[23] Another contributor to the same journal even termed it "counter-revolutionary".[24] Such opinions reinforced the heavy industry-mindedness of many planners and ministerial officials.

Nevertheless the light industrial lobby did have its spokesmen amongst academic advisers and planners as well as party officials and Soviet deputies throughout the period. It was the latter functionaries who made public many light industrial manager's complaints against the All Union ministries. The party's daily *Pravda* (no doubt under Zhdanov's influence) and *Izvestiya*, the newspaper of the Soviets and thus of small-scale local industry, carried many of these complaints.

On the academic front, two debates illustrate both the nature of political conflict in the late Stalin era and the change in leadership priorities at the end of his reign. The first of these was the so-called "Notkin debate". This involved a number of academic economists in what on the surface appeared to be a pleasurable theoretical discussion of the sectoral proportions that should apply during the stage of transition to communism. In practice, however, the debate had very important policy implications, for, according to the official ideology, the USSR was approaching this stage. It is obvious to any student of Marx that an abundance of consumer goods is an essential part of full communism. Yet many Soviet economists in the late 1940s still managed to argue that priority to light industry was *not* a necessary feature of the step from socialism to communism. How Notkin, Petrov and others managed to equate this with Marx's writings is not the relevant point. Their main concern was to influence leadership policy at the time and over the next few years. The device of using academic discussion to do so was one form of the "language of conflict" operating at the time.

The link between academic controversy and Politburo policy was nowhere clearer than in the debates that were organised to prepare for a new textbook on political economy. From 1948 under the guidance of K.V. Ostrovityanov the Institute of Economics of the Soviet Academy of Sciences organised a series of debates aimed at determining the correct line to be followed by this textbook, which would form the basis for the training of the next generation of advisers and officials. The very real debate on sectoral priorities that occurred has been documented else-where.[25] Its outcome was the textbook in the form of Stalin's

Economic Problems of Socialism in the USSR. In an appendix to the work Stalin attacked the errors of the economist Yaroshenko. In so doing he came down firmly on the side of the steel eaters, which was, perhaps, not very surprising at the time of the Korean War. Stalin's position was not simply dictated by his own whim but by the balance of opinion in the Institute of Economics and in the Politburo, which was in turn influenced by the international situation and the decline of the party revivalist and consumerist factions after 1948.

New industries

Similar arguments raged over the development of technologically advanced branches of Soviet industry like non-ferrous metals and chemicals. The 18th Party Congress in 1939 had called for sharp increases in the output of these sectors. The needs of the aircraft and armaments industries in the war had further stimulated demand for their products. Yet the fact is that after the war these sectors were largely ignored. The output targets for several sections of the chemical industry were seriously underfulfilled. In later years Nikita Khrushchev argued that this had set back the technical development of Soviet industry by many years.

The reasons for the low priority given to these branches of industry were the same as those experienced by light industry. Other branch ministries preferred to concentrate on their well-established heavy industrial customers, leaving the Ministries of Non-Ferrous Metals and of Chemicals to fund their own expansion as best they could. Ministerial officials were better educated in the needs of iron and steel, coal-mining and machine-building than of the newer industries. Supplying ministries also had less obvious need for chemicals and new alloys than they had for fuel or machinery.

The late 1940s was also the time of the birth of the computer industry. It was a birth process in which the USSR did not join. To this day the Soviets are probably a decade behind the Americans in computer technology. This gap is largely the product of decisions made in the late Stalin period. The science of cybernetics, without which computers could not be developed was one of the casualties of the *Zhdanovshchina*. One of the spin-offs of the condemnation of Western-style genetics led by T.D. Lysenko (see

Chapter 4) was to inhibit the study of the bases of computer technology. Lysenko won the ear of enough influential members of the Politburo to channel Soviet scientists into non-productive paths. This sphere of economic and scientific policy is one in which the Politburo majority's wishes (and those of Stalin personally) dominated because they intervened in a relatively narrow and specialised sphere. Partly because of this narrowness there were relatively few in high positions willing to defend Lysenko's opponents, particularly in view of Stalin's personal interest. In those relatively few areas of policy where the Generalissimo took a personal interest, most politicians considered it impolitic to oppose him. In the overall context of industrial policy, however, these areas were few. Stalin's personal faculties were beginning to fail from about 1948 and his limited attention was increasingly consumed by matters of foreign policy.

Economic relations with other countries

The linkage between quarrels amongst the leadership and debates amongst their advisors can also be seen in the issues of international economic relations. In the last years of the war itself the Politburo factions were arguing over the best way to take reparations from the defeated powers in Eastern Europe. This issue was closely allied to the "insurrectionist" debate in foreign policy. The party revivalists, notably Zhdanov and Mikoyan, tended to favour the establishment of "joint stock" companies between the USSR and local firms as a way of infiltrating Eastern Europe. The less revolutionary faction wanted to seize assets in their entirety and transport them to the USSR. Initially, until 1947, it was the former line that predominated at least as regards Germany. Thereafter, as communist governments were established in Eastern Europe there was a net flow of funds *into* these countries from the USSR, rather than *vice versa*.

As we shall see in a later chapter, the catalyst for the installation of communist governments in Eastern European capitals in 1947 and 1948 was the Marshall Plan. Faced with the prospect of an increasingly hostile and very rich USA offering substantial aid to countries bordering on the USSR, Stalin's government began to change its attitude towards them. Some governments like those of Czechoslovakia and Yugoslavia, although coming more under communist domination, nevertheless expressed interests in accepting American aid.

The Soviet reaction was to strengthen its hold over these "bloc" countries and also to replace the projected American aid with Soviet help. The USA had even offered the Russians themselves help in their economic recovery. This was a challenge to the communist system that the Politburo could not stomach. In spite of the USSR's own economic problems she began to divert resources towards the reconstruction of the economies of her neighbours. This relationship was formalised by the creation in January 1949 of *Comecon*, the Council for Mutual Economic Assistance. Under Stalin Comecon was an umbrella organisation for coordinating separate trade agreements between Moscow and other socialist governments.

The policy change of 1948 was, therefore, due partly to the impact of events on the international scene but also to the changes in the balance of power in the Kremlin occasioned by Zhdanov's death and to political intrigues within the international communist movement.

The academic reflection of these problems can be found in the controversy over the published views of the economist Varga. He argued that a peaceful transition to a socialist form of economy was possible in capitalist countries. In 1948 his Institute of World Economics and Politics was subordinated to the reformed Institute of Economics of the Academy of Sciences headed by K.V. Ostrovityanov. These events have generally been interpreted as part of the ideological clampdown, known as the "Zhdanov-shchina". In other words Western analysts have tended to assume that all unorthodox views were suppressed in the post-war Stalinist decade.

However, it seems more likely that Varga and his Institute were victims of the change in policy line in 1948 rather than of a general clampdown. That is why Varga was neither arrested nor even dismissed and his Institute not closed down but merely downgraded. They were both allowed to survive to fight another policy battle another day.

Varga's views were really unorthodox only by the standards of the 1930s. In the 1940s Stalin himself had been heard to utter that "Socialism is possible even under an English King".[26] Of course Varga's views did not meet with the approval of the insurrectionists in the Politburo who wanted to foment revolutions abroad.

Zhdanov and his allies, however, could only move against Varga when his policy line actually ran counter to that agreed by the Politburo, that is when the Soviets began to establish communist governments in the countries occupied by the Red Army. By 1948 the main advocate of that policy, Zhdanov, was dead but the international situation dictated that at least some of his policies be continued. Varga probably survived partly because his views were close to those held by Malenkov and Beria in 1945–47 and revived by Khrushchev in his policies of peaceful co-existence after Stalin's death. Of the insurrectionists only Molotov survived to challenge Khrushchev's policies; Malenkov seems actually to have put himself in the anti-insurrectionist camp throughout this period.

The administration of industry

It may be surprising that such basic tenets of Marxism as the revolutionary path to communism could be challenged in this way in the USSR under Stalin. Yet, whilst no one ever claimed to be anti-Marxist or anything but pro-Stalinist, they still managed to challenge another bastion of communist orthodoxy – that the profit motive, the apotheosis of capitalism, had no part to play in a socialist economy. The economist Novozhilov, who is well known for his advocacy of profit-like incentives in Soviet industry in the 1960s, was advancing very similar views under Stalin. In fact he had first put his case forward before the war.

Over the period 1946–50 Novozhilov and other economists began again to argue that the marginal concepts used by Western economists should be employed to evaluate construction projects and factory performance in the USSR.[27] That meant using concepts like "rate of interest" and "profitability", whatever new names Novozhilov might invent for them. To more orthodox economists like P. Mstislavskii and S.G. Strumilin these concepts were nothing but "bourgeois". The only criterion for judging what to produce and where in the socialist economy was that of social and political need.

The debate came to a climax in 1950 when T.S. Khachaturov, a transport economist, summed up the agreed conclusions of his colleagues as follows. Marginal concepts could be used but that political and social considerations could override them if the political leadership so decided. Two years later in a letter to Notkin, Stalin repeated the same compromise. He deemed that profitability "must be taken into consideration both in planning construction and in planning production. This is the ABC of our economic activity at the present stage of development".[28] The official position on this issue was clearly influenced by academic debate in spite of attempts by some officials to stifle it. Ostrovityanov's attacks on the "profitability" school did *not* produce cringing self-criticism from his opponents but a reasoned defence of their position.

The main problems for this type of policy lay (and still lie) in their implementation. The first steps in this were actually taken in Stalin's time. In 1948 prices for many heavy industrial goods were increased in a bid to make these enterprises financially self-sufficient and not reliant on state subsidies. These reforms were partially reversed in 1949 after the removal of their architect Voznesensky. Whatever the reasons for this man's dismissal and later execution it allowed the "statist" Malenkov and his supporters in the heavy industrial ministries to preserve much of the subsidy element in the financing of heavy industry. This made any embarrassing attempt to assess their efficiency and probability extremely difficult.

Yet it was the "party revivalists" who were amongst the leading opponents of such capitalist influences as material incentives to increase efficiency. They favoured an alternative that involved the party apparatus more in stimulating the economy. They were to raise efficiency by use of propaganda techniques aimed at encouraging workers to greater efforts. They filled the press with articles on "socialist competition", telling of the achievements of leading workers in producing several times the average for a shift. Whole groups of thousands of workers apparently wrote to Comrade Stalin promising to produce more and better. Actually much of this was a figment of the propagandists' imagination. There is little evidence that workers were very caught up in this near-repetition of the Stakhanovite campaign of the 1930s. Output per worker rose by about one-third over the Fourth Five Year Plan period and most of that can be attributed to improved supplies of machinery, fuel and raw materials, rather than to greater efforts by the workforce. No doubt the ministries welcomed these campaigns as a means of diverting the energy of party officials into channels where they would not conflict with the ministries' interests.

Zhdanov and his supporters also wanted to strengthen the checking role of the party apparatus, to use it as a means of keeping the ministries in line with the Politburo's wishes. The "party revival" did not long survive Zhdanov's death. The Central Secretariat was reorganised in 1948 under Malenkov's direction to limit its effectiveness as a checker. Even the All Union Central Committee failed to meet at all for four years after Zhdanov's demise. The ministries continued to dominate industrial policy partly because they had very influential advocates in the Politburo in the form of the Malenkov–Beria "statist" faction. It was no coincidence that, after Stalin's death, Malenkov chose to hold the post of Chairman of the Council of Ministers and relinquish that of General Secretary of the party to Khrushchev. Malenkov felt in 1953 that the ministries provided a more substantial base than did the party. Events could also have proved him correct, if Khrushchev had not been able to mobilise the fear the rest of the leadership had of Beria and his secret police.

In Stalin's last decade, therefore, the rigid system of industrial administration developed in the 1930s was never fundamentally altered. Although its shortcomings were becoming more and more obvious by the time of the Fifth Five Year Plan, the advocates of reform lacked sufficient backing at Politburo level seriously to challenge the ministerial machine of the "command" economy.

POLICIES AND POLICY-MAKING IN SOVIET INDUSTRY, 1945–53

The history of Soviet industry over this period is one of initial successes and hopes for fundamental changes, followed by a reassertion of orthodoxy and rigidity. Until 1947 or 1948 industry was being reconverted to civilian needs. In the process the leadership, or at least a working majority within it, was willing to press for more resources to be diverted to the newer regions and branches and to light industry, and to use resources from abroad and to raise efficiency to do so. Thereafter these initiatives seemed to lose their direction in the face of both ministerial obstruction and a changing balance of opinion in the Politburo. This latter change was not particularly of Stalin's making. It was the product of pressures from the international environment as well as from the ministries. It was also associated with the events that followed on the death of Yuri Zhdanov.

Policies in the industrial sphere were not made by Stalin on a personal whim, nor even simply by any dominant faction within his Politburo. The balance of opinion within the leadership was influenced by factors beyond their control like Zhdanov's death, the drought of 1946 and the Marshall Plan. The Politburo's decisions were also influenced by the wide circle of advisors and officials in the Academy of Sciences, in the ministries in Gosplan, and in the party and Soviets. Zhdanov and Molotov (probably backed by Stalin) tried to revive the party's influence to act as a counterweight to the size and power of the ministerial machine. The sources of ministerial power lay in their direct control over the administration of industry and in their supporters in the Politburo, especially Malenkov and Beria.

It was later in his reign that Stalin sought to limit the power of this "statist" faction by downgrading some of its supporters and by promoting its rivals, notably Khrushchev. Yet it was only after the Generalissimo's death that Khrushchev succeeded in reviving the party and defeating the influence of, firstly Beria, then Malenkov and finally Kaganovich and Voroshilov.

None of these factions operated in a vacuum. They were all subject to the influence of their subordinates in the organisations they headed. In addition these factions were not allied in a consistent pattern. At one time the statist Malenkov might find himself in agreement with the party revivalist Molotov (over, for example, the need to raise consumer goods output in 1946). At another they might be fiercely opposed (for example, over the issue of economic relations with Eastern Europe). An economic relations voluntarist like Voznesensky (commonly supposed to have been allied to Zhdanov) may have had quite different views from some party revivalists over, say, the primacy of heavy industry. The balance of opinion within the leadership varied from issue to issue and over time as external circumstances changed.

Stalin often went with the majority of his colleagues. His influence overrode theirs only if he was prepared to make a prolonged and sustained effort to ensure that his wishes were obeyed. He could only do this in a fairly narrow sphere of policy (as in genetics). Even if he had been young and fit he could not have controlled all policy areas in this way. Old and infirm as he was by the late 1940s he had to leave much of the policy-making to his colleagues and subordinates. As long as Soviet industry continued to expand he was perhaps quite willing to do so. In fact industrial output in the USSR did grow rapidly right up until his death in 1953. However this aggregate growth hid serious disproportions between sectors, regions and old and new industries, as well as long-term problems of administration and efficiency. That these issues were not resolved in the Generalissimo's lifetime was not so much his doing as that of the opponents of reform in his leadership and in the state bureaucracy. After his death Khrushchev in particular sought to grapple with these problems but, even under international and economic circumstances that were more favourable than those of the 1940s, he finally had to give way to bureaucratic pressure. Although some of his reforms did survive his removal in 1964, those directed at the economic ministries did not.

4   Agricultural Policy

INTRODUCTION: THE BACKGROUND TO 1945

Agriculture has long been described as the Achilles' heel of the Soviet system. Throughout Russian history the large and backward rural sector has been a matter of grave concern to the country's rulers. The Stalin era is, of course, best known for the brutal collectivisation campaign of 1929–32. By the mid 1930s 99 per cent of the Soviet peasantry had been brought under Moscow's control through the twin systems of collective and state farms. As the pre-war decade developed, so some of the harsher aspects of this system were softened. In 1935 peasants who had been forced into the new large-scale farms were allowed to cultivate in their spare time small private plots of their own land. In 1939 official blessing was given to the establishment of small quasi-independent working units within the collective farms, known as "links" (*zven''ya*). Nevertheless the prices paid by the state to the collectives for their produce remained pitifully low. Workers on both state and collective farms were very poorly paid. The supply of food to the Soviet citizen was barely adequate and the whole agricultural sector remained starved of labour and other resources that were directed towards the industrialisation campaign. The result by 1940 was a rural sector that still employed more than half the Soviet population but was grossly inefficient and generally neglected.

The Nazi invasion reduced Soviet agricultural production to a critical level. By 1942 Hitler's armies occupied nearly half of the USSR's agricultural land and took over the same proportion of its livestock herds. These figures included some of the most fertile land in the country, especially in the Ukraine and the North Caucasus. The German troops, whom some peasants had welcomed as liberators, proved even harsher masters than Stalin's officials had been. Far from abolishing the collective farms the

74

occupying forces exploited them to feed themselves. They also removed most of the able-bodied men, animals and machinery from these farms. During the war the USSR lost, among other things, 7 million (or 60.3 per cent) of its horses, 20 million (or 87 per cent) of its pigs and 137,000 (or 26 per cent) of its tractors. These animals and machines were either taken away, left to rot or die or destroyed. Many agricultural areas suffered fierce fighting in both 1941–42 and 1943–45 when first the invader came and later the Red Army drove him out. Both sides in the conflict employed "scorched earth" policies, devastating whole areas to render them useless to the enemy. There was very little agricultural capital left in the Ukraine and the Northern Caucasus by 1946.

To some extent these losses were made good by exploiting the land and livestock of the central and eastern regions. The leadership lacked the resources to provide more machinery and fertilisers to the farmers in these areas. Farm managers and peasants were encouraged to exploit whatever land they could. Even canteens and factories began to sow crops and vegetables in their gardens. Above all the regime inevitably had to allow the peasants' private plots to flourish. The regulations limiting their size to less than one hectare were not abolished; instead they were allowed to cultivate state- or collectively owned land for their own profit. Indeed one author claims that some Soviet peasants expected the collective farm system to be abolished after the war.[1]

In spite of this laxity and the liberation of many agricultural areas in 1943 and 1944, the net impact of the war was to reduce production levels to well below their (none too high) pre-war levels. Table 4.1 shows the extent of the damage.

TABLE 4.1[2] *Agricultural output, 1936–45*

Year	Total agricultural output (at 1965 prices) (1000 million rubles)	Grain production (million tons)	Meat production (million tons: dead weight)
1936–40 (average)	29.8	77.4	4.0
1940	39.6	95.6	4.7
1945	24.1	47.3	2.6

Even if one ignores the especially good results of 1940 (due to favourable weather conditions), agricultural output in 1945 was at least one-fifth down on pre-war levels. Indeed food supplies had to be supplemented by American aid under the land-lease programme. In addition policy-makers had to cope with a legacy of several years of lax discipline on both state and collective farms. The political departments of the Machine Tractor Stations had been reintroduced in 1941 in a bid to maintain some political control over the agricultural sector. But even they were abolished in 1943.

The issues facing the post-war policy-makers were basically how far to revive Soviet agriculture, and how to do it. Should resources continue to be concentrated on industry or was the time ripe to improve the food supply? If the USSR was to be agriculturally self-sufficient (and no one seriously suggested that it should not be), was this best achieved by pumping more men, machinery and fertilisers into the farming sector or by making more efficient use of what already existed?

Food consumption levels were so low in 1945 that some revival of agricultural output was inevitable. This was especially true after the disastrous mixture of drought and severe winter that was 1946. Although agricultural output as a whole did not fall, the grain harvest was a pitiful 39.6 million tons, some 30 million tons less than was being produced in the last peacetime years of the Tsarist regime! The effect on the livestock sector was felt in 1947. In 1946 cattle and pigs could not be fed because of a shortage of fodder crops and were slaughtered. Meat production thus actually rose by one-fifth in 1946. It fell by the same amount in 1947 as many breeding animals had been killed in the previous year. Although no official statistics were ever published it is known that probably thousands of Soviet citizens died of starvation in 1946.

Policy-makers had to find a way of increasing output rapidly. Building more tractors and providing more fertilisers would increase production only after a year or two as the crop cycle worked its way through. The leadership had to find a way of increasing the efficiency of agricultural production more rapidly in 1946 and 1947. There were broadly two options open to them. The first was to divide the collective and state farms into smaller units and encourage the peasants to work on their own initiative. The alternative was to make the farms even bigger and bring them more firmly under party and state control. The battle between these two lines continued throughout the period until Stalin's death over issues like the "link" system and Khrushchev's plans for giant "agro-towns". At the same time members and their advisers were falling out over whether the level of food production in the USSR was adequate to meet the needs of a population reduced in size by wartime losses or whether it should be further developed. By 1952 Malenkov was arguing that the "grain problem" was solved and Khrushchev that much more needed to be done to boost agricultural production.

In some respects agricultural issues were associated with the battle between factions based on the party and state bureaucracies. The "party revivalist" faction at various times used agricultural failures as an excuse for promoting more party control on the farms. They also promoted the quasi-Marxist agronomic ideas of pseudo-scientists like Lysenko as a way of increasing agricultural yields. The statist faction did not always oppose such moves but was concerned to retain and expand the role of state agencies such as the ministries of Agriculture and of Procurements, against the influence of their party rivals.

In summary agricultural output could be increased by raising efficiency by relying on either smaller or larger-scale farms, by implementing "scientific miracles" on a nationwide scale, or by bringing the whole structure more firmly under the control of either the party or the state bureaucracy. In so far as it is possible to generalise, it seems that the party revivalists (and later Khrushchev and his allies) favoured a regeneration of Soviet agriculture, whilst the Malenkov–Beria axis saw the rural sector as something from which as much as possible had to be procured for a minimum of expenditure of resources. Both factions and their bureaucratic support wanted greater control over agriculture in their own hands to further these contradictory aims.

THE FORMATION AND IMPLEMENTATION OF
AGRICULTURAL POLICY, 1945–53

The priority of the agricultural sector

As has already been indicated 1946 was one of the worst years in
Soviet agricultural history. Officially it was admitted that the
drought was the worst since the 1920s. In practice thousands of
people starved to death. The effects of invasion and the loss of
many skilled workers and machinery would have hit Soviet
agriculture hard in any case. Figures published after Stalin's
death put Soviet agricultural output in 1945 at only 60 per cent of
its (already low) 1940 level, although the population this had to
feed was significantly reduced. Agricultural output per head in
1945 must have been about one-third below its pre-war level.
Most Soviet citizens were living at or near subsistence levels. The
effect of the drought was thus a famine, although only in some
areas of the USSR. According to official (post-Stalin) statistics
agricultural output actually rose overall in 1946, but increases in
some areas could not be moved to others fast enough to avoid
deaths in the Ukraine and neighbouring regions.

Against this background the USSR had little choice but to
continue to accept aid through the United Nations Relief
Administration (UNRA). Receiving food from abroad was,
however, unacceptable to most if not all factions within the Soviet
leadership and bureaucracy. The USSR could hardly retain its
recently won superpower status if it could not feed its population
at least enough to keep them alive.

Beyond this unanimity, there was no agreement on how far the
agricultural sector should be expanded after the war. On the one
hand the USSR continued to export grain to earn hard currency
to pay for industrial imports. At a time of famine this clearly
denotes a low priority to agriculture. Yet at the same time the
Fourth Five Year Plan of April 1946 approved output targets for
agriculture in 1950 that promised a substantial boost for that
sector. It is true that the target increased over 1940 levels was
lower for agriculture than for industry, but then agriculture had
suffered more unrebated losses in the war than industry. In other
words, the 1950 target figure envisaged far more rapid growth in
agriculture than in heavy industry over the period 1945–50 as

Table 4.2 shows. The plan was to restore to agriculture much, but not all, of the ground it had lost to heavy industry during the war.

TABLE 4.2   *The Fourth Five Year Plan targets for Agriculture and Industry*

Sector	Planned output in 1950	
	At 1940 = 100	At 1945 = 100
Industry	148	161
(a) Heavy industry	160	143
(b) Light industry	129	219
Agriculture	127	212

To achieve this some 19.9 billion rubles were to be invested in agriculture by the state, with the *Kolkhozy* themselves being called upon to reinvest about double this figure (although how they were to achieve this was not explained). In addition industry was to deliver $5\frac{1}{2}$ million tons of fertiliser to agriculture in 1950 (compared to just over three million tons in 1940). Over the Five Year Plan period 325 000 tractors were to be built and $4\frac{1}{2}$ billion rubles' worth of machinery delivered to the agricultural sector. In comparison the total stock of tractors in the USSR in 1940 had been only 531 000 and in 1945 397 000.

In summary this plan was far more beneficial to agriculture than most of its predecessors, although much ground had to be made up from wartime losses. The plan was drawn up before the worst climatic effects of 1946 were known. The regime's reaction to the drought came in September 1946 and February 1947. These are key dates in Soviet agricultural policy in this period as they illustrate very clearly that the backing for agricultural development came more from the party than the state apparatus. It was the party machinery that was strengthened to deal with the crisis, not the state's.

In September 1946 the Council of Ministers published a decree *On measures for the liquidation of violations of the Model Statute on Agricultural Cooperatives in the Kolkhozy*.[3] Its aim was to restore discipline to collective farms in which, in wartime, the leadership had allowed peasants to exploit collective machinery, land and livestock for their own profit. Some *Kolkhozy* scarcely deserved the name "collective" by 1946. Now they were being made scapegoats for the agricultural problems of that year.

Most interesting of all from the standpoint of factional politics was the body established to bring the collectives back under central control. It was not the Ministry of Agriculture but the newly-created Council on Kolkhoz Affairs. The exact status of the Council was never made clear. It seems that it was an *ad hoc* organ established for a particular purpose. Once that purpose was achieved it seems to have disappeared. There is certainly no record of its functioning after about 1947 and it was formally abolished in 1953. It is known, however, that it reported to the party leadership: the Politburo and the Central Committee. It was headed by A.A. Andreev who, although he had also been a minister for a few years during the war, was basically a party man. He had been in charge of the party's disciplinary organs as early as 1926 and had been a party secretary continuously since 1935. It was this post that he gave up to chair the Council on Kolkhoz Affairs. Andreev was a key figure in the party revivalist faction.

Indeed the whole spirit of the decree of September 1946 was very much in accord with the party revival. The restoration of collectivity at the expense of individuality was the expression in agriculture of Zhdanov's calls for increasing ideological orthodoxy in the arts. And it was the party (whose secretariat Zhdanov controlled) that was to enforce the orthodoxy. The state administration of agriculture had gradually been fragmented during and immediately after the war. What had previously been under the control of one Ministry of Agriculture had between 1943 and 1946 been split amongst three separate ministries dealing with grain, technical crops and livestock respectively. As a result both state and collective farms were responsible to three different state masters (not to mention the separate Ministry of Procurements!). Coordination of the farming sector was therefore left to the party Central Committee's agriculture department and the Council on Kolkhoz Affairs.

February 1947 seems to mark the zenith of the party revivalists' influence in agriculture. That was the date of the last Central Committee plenum to be held before Stalin's death. What was then and is today a central body in the Soviet political system did not meet again until after the Generalissimo's demise. When it did so it returned to the topic it had dealt with in 1947 – agriculture.

The February 1947 plenum called for "such an expansion of agriculture that will in a very short time permit the creation of an abundance of food for our populace, of raw materials for light industry and for laying down the necessary state reserves of food and raw materials".[4] This was no empty promise. Although much of the decree was devoted to calls for better administration and the restoration of *Kolkhoz* discipline, it also made more concrete moves to increase output.

The party leadership now demanded that the Five Year Plan's targets for agriculture should not simply be fulfilled but over-fulfilled. This was to be achieved firstly by expanding the areas under crop in 1947 and 1948. 12.4 million hectares of extra land were to be ploughed up and planted with grain. The areas devoted to other crops were to be expanded by between 18 and 70 per cent in two years. Some of this was land that had been neglected (or used for illegal private purposes) during the war. But particular note was also made of targets to expand land use in the eastern regions of the USSR (an early indication of the ideas behind Khrushchev's "Virgin Lands" scheme of 1954–55).

The plenum also demanded that herds of livestock should regain their pre-war levels by 1948 or 1949, targets that were well above those for *1950* announced a year before in the Five Year Plan.

This "new deal" in agriculture was to be achieved by improving yields as well as by ploughing up more land and breeding more cattle and pigs. A key role in this was to be played by the Machine Tractor Stations (MTSy). The MTS not only performed mechanised work for the collective farms, it also provided them with advice and assistance as to better quality seeds, fodder and so on and better crop rotations. Its main political significance, however, was as the party and state's main link with the collective farms. The farms had to pay the MTSy for their work in kind. This is a vital part of the state system of procuring agricultural produce from the farms.

In contrast to industry where the factories were state-owned and each had its own party and state organisation, the *Kolkhozy* were legally speaking independent cooperatives. Many had no formal party organisation. The MTS was, for such farms, their main day-to-day link with the state and party apparatus. Although the state formally controlled the MTSy they were also a key part of party strategy. Whilst there were no primary party organisations (PPOs) on many *Kolkhozy* (and so no party presence at all), most MTSy had one. In fact the plenum reintroduced to the MTS the post of Deputy Director (Political) or *Zampolit*.

The Zampolit was responsible to the relevant regional party organisation.

He was expected to spend much of his time in the fields encouraging the collective farm workers and managers to embrace new techniques – new types of seed, different crop rotations and so on. A 1950 survey of the working month of one *Zampolit* showed him spending over half his time on the collective farms actually in the fields.[5] This example was quoted with approval. The party saw the MTS (each of which dealt with at least three or four *Kolkhozy*) as their main means of promoting agricultural development at grass roots level. This development, they hoped, could be achieved in part by spreading agronomic knowledge amongst the collectives. If the Ministry of Agriculture was too slow in doing it, then the party could press for it through the *Zampolity*.

At the same time as this combined revival of agriculture and the party there were also moves to restructure the state bureaucracy. Days before the February 1947 plenum the old Ministry of Agriculture had been restored to its previous form – controlling all the collectives with a separate ministry responsible for the state farms. Within the Ministry of Agriculture control of the MTSy was now centred on one *glavk*. In spite of the party revival the state lobby was able to regain some of its lost ground in the policy formation process.

According to most Kremlinologists the party revival came to an end with the death of Zhdanov in 1948 and the subsequent purging of many of his supporters, notably Kuznetsov and Voznesenskii. In the agricultural context, however, there was clearly still a strong lobby pressing for more priority to be given to the production of foodstuffs. In 1948 and 1949 ambitious schemes were announced to protect and improve the land by planting forestry belts and by massive irrigation schemes and to rebuild the livestock sector. Some of these schemes can be linked to the party revivalists. Even after Zhdanov's death some prominent party men like Andreev retained their influence amongst the leadership. Even when Andreev's star faded in 1950, he had in a sense already been superseded by Khrushchev who had been moved to Moscow by Stalin in 1949 specifically to counteract the power of Malenkov, Beria and the "statists". Khrushchev was and remained, above all, a party man. He had always held party posts; what had changed since the 1930s was his obsession with agriculture, which had developed during his years in charge of the Ukrainian republic (which he left only in 1949). The party apparatus was thus, throughout Stalin's last decade, associated with the promotion of rural development.

Many of the grandiose schemes for transforming Soviet agriculture that were approved at this time have been treated by Western analysts as little more than "window dressing". They argue that, for example, the "Stalin Plan" of October 1948 was never intended as anything more than an exercise in propaganda. Yet this plan, like all those aimed at giving the rural sector a higher priority, dealt in specific plan targets, actual figures for lower officials to aim at and for providing them with the necessary materials. The plans were ambitious, but they were issued not simply for foreign consumption, but also as instructions from the party leadership to lesser officials of the party and the state. The fact that many of these plans were not realised was not simply due to their being unrealistic in the first place. It was also due to the reluctance of many state authorities to give the necessary priority to the party-backed form of agricultural expansion.

From the spring of 1948 Stalin's leadership embarked on a series of plans to update and mechanise Soviet agriculture. In May of that year the Council of Ministers approved a decree for the further electrification of the Soviet countryside over the years 1948–50. It went so far as to make rural electrification as the "most important" means of increasing labour productivity in the *Kolkhozy*, the state farms and the MTSy".[6] In three years the number of *Kolkhozy* with electricity was to treble and 4300 MTSy and 3724 *Sovkhozy* (state farms) were to be similarly equipped. Specific ministries were obliged to build new power stations (even the rate per year being specified). Furthermore all kinds of state organisations in Moscow and in the regions were called upon to provide the equipment for this programme and schedules for training power workers were announced. This amount of detail showed a clear intention. Even if all targets were not met, the leadership were giving a high priority to agriculture, not simply indulging in fantasising.

The most famous of all these schemes was the so-called "Stalin Plan for the Transformation of Nature".[7] Its grandiose title belies the fact that it applied to only some of the agricultural regions of the USSR, notably the Trans Volga, the North Caucasus and the central Black Earth regions, all to the south of Moscow. The plan was designed to combat soil erosion in these areas and thus prevent disasters like the 1946 drought recurring in the future. The main thrust of the plan was the planting of gigantic forests in strips that would protect these areas from wind erosion. In addition large scale irrigation schemes were to be introduced. Finally the system of grasslands rotations which had been promoted ever since the war was to be further developed. The impact of the shelter belts, irrigation and grasslands schemes would, it was hoped, raise yields of grain by 20–30 per cent (with greater increases for other crops) within 3–5 years, as well as preventing enormous losses from droughts.[8]

This was of necessity a long-term programme. The shelter belts were not scheduled to be completed until 1965. Nevertheless the decree gave clear instructions that some of the projects were to be put into operation in 1949, 1950 and 1951 and that a special organisation directly subordinate to the Council of Ministers be set up to coordinate the work involved. Hundreds of nurseries were to be set up within two years to provide the trees for these shelter belts.

The Stalin plan in effect gave a further priority to agriculture in that it enshrined a particular approach to the problem. As we shall see later in this chapter, the idea that Soviet agriculture could be revolutionised by using more modern technology to tame the environment was associated with a particular school of thought. Most prominent amongst these were V.R. Vil'yams and T.D. Lysenko and his Lenin Agricultural Institute (*VASKhNIL*).[9] Lysenko was opposed by Zhdanov and his party revivalists. The Plan thus fitted into the revivalist strategy in agriculture only up to a point and was probably backed by figures in both state and party factions. It was largely organs of state that were charged with implementing it. The attaching of Stalin's name to it did not necessarily mean that he had initiated it. It did mean that he approved of it and that thus all had to appear to agree with the plan and be working for its execution.

In the following year, 1949, it was the turn of the livestock sector to benefit from the Politburo's attention. A Three Year Plan was announced with the aim of restoring herds of cattle, pigs, sheep and goats and horses to something like their pre-war levels. In actuality the plan targets for 1952 were very little above those for 1950 announced in the Fourth Five Year Plan (as Table 4.3 shows). However, they did imply significant increases over the period 1949–52 as the Five Year Plan was to that date not being fulfilled.

TABLE 4.3   *Livestock herds in the USSR*[10]

	(million head at 1 Jan) 1941	1946	Five Year Plan for 1951	Actual 1951	Three Year Plan for 1953
Cattle	54.8	47.6	65.3	57.1	69.7
Sheep and goats	91.7	70.0	121.5	99.0	139.0
Pigs	27.6	10.6	31.2	24.4	31.0
Horses	21.1	10.7	15.3	13.8	16.5

The Three Year Plan therefore commanded that a new priority be given to the livestock sector over this period.

Stalin's Politburo did not therefore ignore the needs of Soviet agriculture. They sought to develop it by pumping resources into one sector and then another, by mechanising, irrigating, use all the latest agronomic advances. What they would not do, however, was to give the collective farmers more incentive to work better by paying them more for their produce. Most *Kolkhozniki* made next to nothing from their work for the collective; the state compulsorily purchased ("procured") most of their output at ludicrously low prices. The collective farm worker could only survive by growing what he could for himself and selling some of it on the local market. When Khrushchev suggested that higher prices should be paid, he records that he received a complete rejection from Stalin personally.[11]

Paradoxically this did not mean that Stalin's Politburo had refused to give any priority to agriculture. Their whole aim had been to develop this sector to produce more food for the population without making the peasantry any richer. Stalin's regime's relationship with the Soviet rural citizen had never been less than suspicious; at worst it had been very bloody. The Politburo of his last decade were prepared to pay for agricultural development but they wanted the funds to go to state organisations like the MTSy, the forestry stations, the power stations and the state farms, not to the collective farms.

As we have seen in the previous chapter it was one thing for the leadership to announce plans and decrees and allot funds and resources to programmes and quite another for those to be carried out through the labyrinths of the state bureaucracy. Most of the initiatives on the rural sector can be traced to the party-based factions. Even Khrushchev's 1952 plea for increased prices came from that source. At the time he was Stalin's leading agricultural specialist in the Central Committee's secretariat, as well as being First Secretary of the Moscow *obkom*, which is a significant agricultural producer.

Of necessity the party relied on the state to carry out the plans. The extent to which the various plans were fulfilled reveals that the state often failed to obtain its targets and yet few if any of its agents suffered for this failure. The attitude of certain state officials to the agricultural situation was best summed up by Malenkov's complacent statement to the 19th Party Congress 1952 that the "grain problem" no longer existed; this in spite of the fact that the 1952 grain harvest was still less than the 1940 level. According to Khrushchev, Malenkov had been the party's nominal agricultural "expert" back in 1947;[12] yet, by Stalin's own admission, Malenkov knew nothing about agriculture. Furthermore his background and affiliations put him far more in the "statist" camp. Khrushchev's later reminiscences are full of Malenkov and Beria's opposition to his plans to develop agriculture. After Khrushchev's complaints to Stalin about the Ukrainian famine in 1946, the former was actually demoted from his party secretaryship of the Ukraine, albeit only for a few months. Nevertheless the influence of the party faction (and of Khrushchev's own protestations to Stalin) was strong enough to get the 1947 plenum convened and to restate the priority for agriculture.

Although the party lobby managed to get leadership approval for all of these programmes to develop agricultural output and productivity at a time when the targets for most sectors of industry were fulfilled, or, in many cases, overfulfilled. Aggregate agricultural production in 1950 was 20 per cent short of its Five Year Plan target and marginally below its 1940 level. The years 1951 and 1952 saw very little improvement on this level. Output in 1952 was 1 per cent above its 1940 level. The fulfilment of other output plans is shown in Table 4.4. Of course most of these achievements represented substantial improvements over 1945 production levels but, with the exception of cotton, most of the production targets in arable farming were not met by a long way. The output plans for livestock produce were never published, but it seems clear that they were underfulfilled although probably by a lesser margin than for crops.

TABLE 4.4 *Fulfilment of Five Year Plan for Agriculture*[13]

Sector	Planned output in 1950	Actual output in 1950	% Fulfilment of Plan
All Agricultural Output (at 1940 = 100)	127	99	80
Grain (mil tons)	101.6[a]	81.2	80
Sugar Beet (mil tons)	26	20.8	80
Raw Cotton (mil tons)	3.1	3.54	114
Flax (mil tons)	0.8	0.255	32
Sunflower Seeds (mil tons)	3.7	1.8	49

NOTE
[a] This is an estimated barn yield target (see note 13).

The reason for these shortfalls is not to be found in poor supplies of state aids in the form of machinery, electrification, forestry belts, fertilisers and so on. In spite of enormous wartime losses the agricultural sector actually had 12 per cent more tractors and 16 per cent more combine harvesters in 1950 than in 1940.[14] The ambitious Five Year Plan to provide agriculture with $5\frac{1}{2}$ million tons of fertiliser in 1950 (compared to a little over three million tons in 1940) was 97 per cent fulfilled. The demand for electrical energy in agriculture was nearly three times as high as in 1940. It is not possible to assess the fulfilment of the 1948 decree on electrification, but it did give agriculture an enormous boost in this respect.

The Plan for the Transformation of Nature envisaged that an average of about 350 000 hectares of forestry belts would be planted per year over the period 1949–65. In practice more than double this area was planted in both 1950 and 1951.[15] The plan was actually over-fulfilled in the Stalin era. By 1951 more than two million hectares of the total of 5.7 million had already been planted.

The regime also kept its promises to agriculture in the sphere of training specialists to work on and assist farms with new technology. The number of trained agronomists in Soviet agriculture nearly tripled over the period 1941–53 and grew especially in the Kolkhoz and MTS sector, despite many wartime losses.

The leadership thus ploughed at least as many resources into agriculture as it had planned in most respects. Yet this mechanical and technical revolution did not produce the effect on output that the leadership hoped for. One of the main reasons for this was that there were not enough workers and administrators on the farms and that they were not using the new technology very efficiently. In the case of arable farming, although sufficient areas were sown, the yields of crops were in most cases (the major exception being cotton) still below pre-war levels in 1950 and well short of their plan targets. In livestock farming there was a consistent failure to build up the herds at the rate demanded in leadership directives.

Plan fulfilment in these respects is detailed in Tables 4.5 and 4.6.

In view of the increased availability of technical advice, machinery, electricity and so on why did the MTSy and the farms not make better use of the land and build up herds of cattle and pigs? Part of the answer is that many of the facilities needed to operate the machinery, such as drivers and spare parts for tractors, were in very short supply. The other part is that most of the "aid" from the state was channelled through the MTSy and similar organisations, with whom most *Kolkhozy* were reluctant to deal for both financial and political reasons.

Soviet agriculture lost many of its able-bodied young men, especially those who could drive or operate machinery, to the war effort. In total the *Kolkhozy* (who bore the brunt of this sacrifice) had lost about one-fifth of their workforce over the period 1940–45. Even by 1950 there were only 27.6 million working in the whole agricultural sector compared to 29 million in 1940. In spite of training many women to drive and operate machinery during the war the collectives and the MTSy still had fewer skilled operatives in 1940 than in 1950. Life in the Soviet countryside at this time was simply not rewarding enough to attract young people, especially from the towns and from the army. Workers on both *Kolkhozy* and *Sovkhozy* earned precious little from their work for the state and had to compensate this by developing their own small private plots. Taxes on these plots were increased at least twice during this period. Even the MTS-trained operatives did not seem very keen on their lifestyle. The rapid turnover of labour on

TABLE 4.5 *Sown areas in the USSR*[16]

Crop	Area sown in 1945	1947 Plenum Plan for 1948	Five Year Plan for 1950	Area sown in 1950	Fulfilment of Five Year Plan (%)
			Million Hectares		
Grain	85.3	N.A.	105.8	102.9	97
Sugar Beet	0.83	1.32	1.37	1.31	96
Cotton	1.21	1.53	1.68	2.32	138
Flax	1.00	1.58	2.00	1.90	95
Potatoes	8.30	9.11	N.A.	8.60	–
Vegetables	1.80	2.00	N.A.	1.30	–

TABLE 4.6 *Livestock herds in USSR*[17]

	1947 Plenum Plan	1 Jan. 1949 Actual	Fulfilment percentage	Five Year Plan	1 Jan. 1951 Actual	Fulfilment percentage	Three Year Plan	1 Jan. 1953 Actual	Fulfilment percentage
Cattle	56.1	54.8	98	65.3	57.1	87	69.7	56.6	81
incl. Cows	27.2	24.2	89	27.2	24.3	89	31.5	24.3	77
Sheep & Goats	97.8	85.6	88	121.5	99.0	81	139.0	109.9	79
Pigs	20.3	15.2	75	31.2	24.4	78	31.0	28.5	92
Horses	12.9	11.8	91	15.3	13.8	90	16.5	15.3	93

the MTSy was a source of frequent concern in the press and at public meetings.[18] Even if rural workers could earn reasonable wages there was little in the local shops upon which to spend their money.

The effect of the labour shortage was that some machinery was left idle for lack of people to work it. Many MTS operatives also showed little concern for how well they did their work. Another common complaint was of tractor and combines standing idle for lack of spare parts and fuel.

One collective farm chairman from the Ukraine describes how he and other managers had to resort to bribery, black-market dealings and even outright theft to obtain vitally needed parts for their machines.[19] Machinery was often abused and thereby damaged, especially by MTS operatives. Tractors and combines were often left out of doors in all weathers!

The relationship between the *Kolkhoz* and the MTS was a major cause of the poor performance of Soviet agriculture at this time. The collectives formed the bulk of the farming sector. They had ten times the number of workers on the state farms. Stalin's leadership, as we have seen, wanted to regenerate the *Kolkhozy* through the MTSy rather than by giving resources direct to the farms themselves. By this they hoped to enhance party and state control over the collectives and to "industrialise" them by electrification, mechanisation and so on (and thus increase yields). Furthermore the collectives had to pay the MTS in kind. The *Kolkhoz* gave the MTS produce in exchange for the work done in its fields. These payments-in-kind were valued at state procurement prices that were often well below free market prices or even production costs. A greater role for the MTS thus meant more (low-priced) procurements for the state to distribute in the towns.

In practice, however, most collectives tried to keep all contact with the MTSy to a minimum for both economic and political reasons. They had to pay through the nose for all MTS work, even having to pay for some repairs to MTS machinery. They had little control over how the work was done. In fact in general the state agencies that supplied items to the collectives seemed to take very little responsibility for their actions. The same chairman ("Belov") tells us how his deliveries of fertiliser were habitually left at the wrong railway station and were stored in the open air, rendering a third of the delivery useless!

Party and state authorities generally were more interested in fulfilling the letter of the plan than its intent. Belov was once reprimanded and his farm deprived of scarce supplies because he refused to sow his sugar beet at the time demanded by the local organs of state. The sugar refinery wanted planting to begin early because it had the seeds ready and wanted the beet as early as possible to help it fulfil its output plan. In this it was backed up by the local agriculture department which wanted to show higher authority that *its* area was well ahead with its sowing plan. Only the *Kolkhoz* chairman (and, for once, the MTS agronomist) agreed that the weather was simply too cold for planting![20] No wonder farms preferred to keep their dealings with the organs of Soviet power to a minimum. This preference was also backed up by a history of peasant resentment against the communist regime in general and Stalin's collective system in particular.

Of course the September 1946 decree had sought to clamp down on many of the ways in which collective farm workers and managers evaded regulations. Yet, after a reasonably successful campaign to limit the use of *Kolkhoz* land for private profit, the level of state and party control in the *Kolkhozy* was still totally inadequate to achieve the party revivalists' aim of revolutionising Soviet agriculture. The chaos and illegality that made up much of Belov's working week was by no means confined to the Ukraine in the immediate post-war years. Six months after Stalin's death Khrushchev detailed the shortcomings of Soviet agriculture to the party's Central Committee. He singled out the MTSy as one of the main culprits for the poor agricultural performance of Stalin's last decade; five years later he succeeded in having them abolished altogether. His 1953 report also showed how far the September 1946 decree had not been enforced because the state and party machinery to do so was lacking and because there was precious little incentive for most farms to raise output. Indeed some farms deliberately understated their production to keep down the level of procurements demanded of them by the state.

Yet several attempts were made after the war to reform the administration of agriculture in a bid either to give farms more incentive to produce more or bring them more under central control to force them to increase their yields and expand their output.

Reforming the administration of Soviet agriculture

Most of the early post-war reforms in this area were piecemeal efforts. The establishment of the Council on Kolkhoz Affairs, for example, was a temporary expedient to iron out some of the inheritance of wartime and to give a public response to the 1946 famine. It seems to have lasted less than a year. Similarly cuts in the number of administrative personnel in the ministries and the restoration of the *Zampolit* on the MTS were not basic reforms of the system of agricultural control, although both represented facets of the party revival.

The two major controversies of the period, concerned Andreev's "link" system and Khrushchev's campaign to amalgamate *Kolkhozy*. The first was an attempt to decentralise Soviet agriculture, which came to an abrupt halt in February 1950. The second was officially approved only three months later and entailed greater centralisation of control over agriculture.

The case of the "*zveno*" or "link" system demonstrates that "decentralisation" and "incentive" were not necessarily prohibited concepts in Stalin's Russia. As in industry these and other proposals for lessening the burden on the collectives were put forward by party and state officials and experts. Indeed, in agriculture these suggestions were not only made but adopted as official policy.

Links are small teams of five or more workers who combine together to cultivate a particular area of land or herd of livestock. To the extent that they are allowed to work independently of *Kolkhoz*, party or state control they operate more like the family smallholding than a collective and greatly increase the individual's incentive to produce. At the height of the controversy over them in the Khrushchev era, some condemned them as a form of decollectivisation and a restoration of private property. In the Stalin era, however, they were for many years officially encouraged, albeit in a rather less independent form.

In fact links had first been tried in the 1930s in the cultivation of non-grain crops, especially sugar beet. They were officially approved at the 18th Party Congress in 1939. Their main advocate then was Andreev. When he assumed overall party responsibility for agriculture after the war, some extension of their use seemed probable. Throughout 1947 a debate raged in the Soviet press over whether links were suitable for grain farming. It was the party apparatus which, not surprisingly, took the lead in promoting grain *zven''ya*. For example, the first secretary of the Kursk *obkom* reported in the party's journal[21] that such links had been tried in his province in 1947 and had secured excellent results. He did, however, criticise the system by which these teams were paid according to how much work they did rather than the amount of grain they harvested. He also indulged in a long attack on the poor work of a number of local MTSy.

It was the MTSy (and thus the state apparatus) that were the main opponents of the link. They argued that small teams were unsuitable for cultivating grain where machinery could be economically used only on larger areas controlled by brigades.

In April 1948 a Council of Ministers decree recommended the adoption of links in non-grain crops and "where possible" also in grain farming. This spirit of compromise between the party and MTS factions was continued by firstly allowing the brigade to remain as the basic form of intra-*Kolkhoz* organisation, with links within them, and secondly by limiting the independence of the teams.[22] On the other hand link members were to be paid according to the amount harvested, rather than the work done, favouring the "party" approach on giving team members a greater interest in the end product of their work. This payment by results was viewed by some as a covert form of profit-sharing.

The implementation of this decree varied widely. Where the local party favoured it (as in Kursk) links became the norm and some had even more independence than the decree allowed.[23] In other areas, especially where the MTS were stronger and better equipped, *zven''ya* failed to gain a foothold in grain farming.

Only two years after this decree both Andreev and his major allies were forced to confess their sins in public. Most links were disbanded. It seems that many teams had come into conflict with the MTS creating a situation that Khrushchev later described as "two masters in one field". It was no coincidence that two years later Stalin himself publicly attacked two economists for suggesting that the MTSy be disbanded and their machinery sold to the *Kolkhozy*.[24]

Yet it is significant that this proposal could in fact be made at this time and furthermore that debate on the issue continued.[25] In addition a number of links continued to exist and lasted until the revival of the link in 1958 (when the MTSy were abolished). Even Stalin's personal intervention could not stamp them out entirely.

It is noteworthy that Andreev, although disgraced, remained chairman of the Party Control Commission for a further two years and was not arrested.

If links were the brainchild of the party's fallen star Andreev, their opposite was the aim of its rising star Nikita Khrushchev. He wanted to increase the size of the basic agricultural unit rather than make it smaller. His proposal for the amalgamation of *Kolkhozy* was adopted in a resolution of the party's Central Committee (although the decree was probably the work of Khrushchev's Secretariat department, not the committee itself) in May 1950. Some collectives had already been merged in order to make them of a size more suited to exploitation by modern machinery. The aim of the amalgamation policy was thus to modernise the farms, but also to bring them more under party control. The larger but fewer *Kolkhozy* each had a chairman who was better qualified than those of the smaller farms and who was also a party man. In Belov's area all the new chairmen were on the party's *raion* committee. In 1946 less than 15 per cent of collective farms had any form of party organisation; their only link with the party was with the MTS. Ten years later more than 80 per cent of the collectives had a party organisation. The amalgamation campaign gave the party more control over agriculture and, in doing so, removed one of the main reasons for maintaining the MTS structure.

The MTSy had originally been built to increase central control over the *Kolkhozy* and also to modernise and mechanise them. One MTS would do the mechanised work for several collectives each of which was too small to make the best use of tractors, combines and so on. The amalgamation reduced the number of *Kolkhozy* in the USSR from 236 900 in 1940 to 93 300 in 1953. Some of the new farms were large enough to utilise machinery to capacity by themselves. Another reason for the continuation of the MTS structure was thus removed.

Although the link and the amalgamation campaign appeared to be contradictory policies, they were both advocated by the party and opposed by the MTSy and their superior, the Ministry of Agriculture. In the final years of Stalin's rule, however, the Ministry and the Malenkov–Beria faction in the Politburo succeeded in halting the party's drive in agriculture. Stalin's rejection of the plan to sell MTS machinery (see note 24) to the *Kolkhozy* was a victory for this group. A better known case is the rejection of Khrushchev's "agrotown" proposals in March 1951. Khrushchev publicly argued for an extension of the *Kolkhoz* amalgamation campaign to create agricultural towns in the centre of giant *Kolkhozy*.[26] This proposal was rejected after pressure by Malenkov and Beria. Malenkov singled out Khrushchev's plan for attack at the 19th Party Congress in October 1952, on the grounds that, in effect, it was too concerned with the interests of the collective farm workers themselves rather than the state.

In most respects, therefore, it was the party that wanted to reform Soviet agricultural administration. In so doing it had an eye on the fact that this could only really be done by improving standards of living on the farms. The incentives of small work teams paid by results, of Khrushchev's suggested higher prices for agricultural produce and of the agrotown idea were all based on this philosophy. They were, however, resisted (in the end successfully) by the state apparatus who wished to preserve the system of agricultural control based on the MTSy and the Ministry of Agriculture.

The other significant development in this period in the administration of agriculture was the collectivisation of the new areas of Latvia, Lithuania, Estonia, Moldavia and of the Ukraine. These had been incorporated into the USSR in the 1940s and lost again in the war. By 1944 they were back in Soviet hands, still with a privately owned agricultural system. In 1947 the policy of "fully voluntary" collectivisation of these areas was announced. By 1950 it was complete but far from voluntary. These new western areas seem to have been collectivised with the same brutality that the rest of the USSR had experienced between 1929 and 1933. In 1951 political departments were established in the MTSy in these areas to ensure party control over the farms, just as they had operated in the rest of the country in 1933/34. There seems to have been no disagreement over this policy within the Politburo. It was so similar to Stalin's own campaign of 20 years before that opposition could easily have been construed as a personal attack on the Generalissimo. When Stalin intervened so directly a matter had high priority and the policies were enforced. When he did not the party and the state battled for control. The main sufferer in this battle was the *Kolkhoz* sector itself. Peasant living standards and agricultural output began to recover only after Stalin's death under the guidance of Khrushchev.

The scientific "revolution" in agriculture and leadership policy

Any analysis of Soviet agriculture in Stalin's last decade cannot ignore the various scientific "miracles" that were advocated as panaceas for Soviet agricultural ills and often adopted as official policy. Most prominent among these were the grasslands system of crop rotation, the campaign for winter wheat and the adoption of shelter belts. Some of these ideas were based on sound agronomic principles and some were not. Yet the effectiveness of them all was limited by the way in which they were introduced in all areas of the country, regardless of their suitability to local climatic and soil conditions.

The idea of introducing crop rotations of up to ten years with perennial grass as one of the crops was associated with the agronomist V.R. Vil'yams. It was intended to provide more fodder for livestock (by growing grass rather than leaving the land fallow) and also to increase the fertility of the soil. This "grasslands" system was officially sanctioned in the Five Year Plan in 1946, by the 1947 plenum and in the 1948 plan for the Transformation of Nature. Western experts agree that the system is sound enough for areas of high rainfall. Yet in the USSR it was applied indiscriminately, even in drier areas where it was of little use. This was done on the direct orders of the leadership.

Stalin himself personally intervened in the matter of spring wheat. Under the influence of the agronomist T.S. Maltsev he forced Khrushchev to expand spring wheat cultivation in the Ukraine, an area more suited to winter wheat.[27] Stalin also promoted the strange theories of T.D. Lysenko and his Lenin Institute. Many of these were based on applying Marxism to genetics. For example, Lysenko claimed that winter wheat seeds could be made more like the higher-yielding spring wheat if their early environment were changed by soaking them and allowing them to sprout before sowing. According to Belov, whose farm had to employ this method in 1948, the seeds simply died![28] Nevertheless Lysenko continued to be regarded as an authority in such matters.

The planting of forestry belts created more problems than it solved in some areas. It was intended to prevent wind erosion of the soil. In practice it split up large fields and made ploughing more complicated and costly. The shelter belts also acted as "breeding grounds for crop-destroying insects".[29]

Many of these agricultural experiments were backed by elements in both the party and the state. Maltsev had strong party connections, yet Lysenko was backed by the statist faction. Stalin himself also seems to have approved many of these experiments. They offered the attraction of low-cost improvements in yields without having to put any more state money in the collective farmer's pocket. The high priority given to them by Stalin's personal role and the statist faction's involvement in their promotion dictated their large-scale implementation. This included the most unsuitable areas. As a result even the better of these schemes did not produce the increased yields claimed of them.

AGRICULTURAL POLICY AND POLICY-MAKING, 1945–53

Stalin's last decade was not an era in which agriculture was ignored. The General Secretary himself took a keen interest in several aspects of agricultural policy. This sector, still dominated by the collective ownership system, received more tractors, fertilisers, electricity and agronomic advice than ever before. The relatively poor results achieved were due partly to the party leadership's reluctance to give the collective farmer greater incentives to work well. The *Kolkhozy* generally had so few funds that such bonuses as were allowed often could not be paid. On the one hand the Politburo would not sanction higher prices for *Kolkhoz* produce that would give the collectives more to work for. On the other hand they sought to discourage the *Kolkhoznik* from working on his own private plot by a series of crippling tax increases. Neither would they reform the structure of agriculture to make the peasant's pay more dependent on how well he worked. The link system, the one exception to this, was allowed in the cultivation of the nation's major crop (grain) for only two years.

The accuracy of this analysis is shown by the case of cotton-growing. This sector outstripped all others at the time overfulfilling the Five Year Plan target by 14 per cent. The cotton-growing farms of Central Asia were often referred to in the Soviet press as "millionaire *Kolkhozy*". For some reason cotton procurements were paid for by the state at prices that were high enough to allow these farms to make a profit. Cotton was also one of the crops which could be cultivated by small links long before the 1948 decree.

Many of the policy initiatives to develop agriculture came directly from the party apparatus. Initially they were the work of the Party Revivalists with A.A. Andreev taking a leading role even after Zhdanov's death. Even before Andreev's disgrace Khrushchev had been called to the Moscow party to act as Stalin's main agricultural adviser. Many of the party's initiatives were approved by Stalin personally. Largely because of this personal intervention they were implemented by both the party and the state apparatus to the letter.

All too often, however, it was the letter and not the spirit of these policies that was enacted. Farms received machinery, electricity and new types of seed as well as orders on how to improve yields. Yet they often lacked the skilled labour, spare parts and fuel to utilise the machinery and the transport to collect their supplies. They were also forced to fulfil programmes like those for "improving" seeds or planting trees that were inapplicable to the needs of their area.

The state agencies dealing with agriculture continued to treat the sector as a poor relation to industry. The Ministries of Agriculture and Procurements, in spite of frequent attacks on their performance, seemed to view the *Kolkhoz* sector as something from which the MTSy should try to expropriate as much produce as possible in return for a minimum of work. The MTS was notoriously inefficient, but it continued to serve a political purpose in spite of frequent public attacks on it. Other state agencies like the Ministries of Agricultural Machine-Building and of the Chemical Industry broadly fulfilled their obligations to agriculture on paper but in practice their work left much to be desired.

These attitudes corresponded to Malenkov and Beria's attempts to prevent too many resources being poured into agriculture at the expense of heavy industry. Whilst the party factions appeared to play a role in the formation of agricultural policy until about 1950 they did not control its implementation well enough. Khrushchev later complained that Stalin had a totally inaccurate idea of the situation on the collectives based on propaganda films showing happy peasants living in warm houses and eating huge joints of meat. In practice there was virtually no meat in some areas and often more food in the towns than on the farms where it was produced. It is possible that Stalin chose to believe these films because it suited his long-held distrust of the Russian peasant. Whichever was the case, he certainly backed the agricultural lobby until Andreev's disgrace in February 1950. Thereafter Khrushchev enjoyed a degree of influence over policy-making. By March 1951, however, Malenkov and Beria had recovered much of their lost ground. For the last two years of Stalin's life agriculture received very little attention from the Politburo. The result was the sorry state of neglect that many farms were in by the time Khrushchev began his crusade to renovate them in September 1953. At the end of Stalin's reign it was the Statist faction and the MTS structure that dominated both the formation and the implementation of Soviet agricultural policy.

5 Foreign Policy

INTRODUCTION

The main issue in Soviet foreign policy has always been the debate between revolution and retrenchment. The zealots of the communist movement in the USSR and elsewhere have argued for the export of revolution. In the 1940s, as today, the Kremlin had its advocates of Soviet aid to revolutionary movements wherever in the world they appeared. Against them ranged the moderates who saw the essential aim of Russian foreign policy as defending the USSR against external aggression not by overthrowing hostile governments but by reaching an accommodation with them.

The Bolshevik revolution of October 1917 was based on the revolutionary ideal. One of the main reasons for Lenin's popularity at the time was his promise to end the costly war against the German Kaiser. To the communists it was an imperialist conflict wagered in the interests of monarchs and businessmen, not workers and peasants. Within six months of coming to power the communists had concluded the Treaty of Brest Litovsk, by which Russia ceded huge tracts of territory to Germany in exchange for an end to hostilities. On the face of it this action smacks of retrenchment rather than revolution; Lenin accommodated his enemies rather than opposed them. If one probes deeper, however, it is clear that his policies were based on an assumption that in the aftermath of war the workers of Germany, Britain, France and elsewhere would rise up and overthrow their masters and help, not hinder the new regime in Petrograd.

Although revolutions were attempted in, for example, Germany and Hungary in 1918, the consequences of Brest Litovsk for the Bolsheviks were counter to what they had hoped. Britain, France and their allies sought the overthrow of Lenin's government. Troops were despatched to the north and south of Russia to help the White armies in their bid to remove the new regime. This unsuccessful intervention in the Civil War might have been expected to reinforce revolutionary rather than retrenchment ideology amongst the Soviet leaders. Yet within six years of the end of the Civil War retrenchment had become the official policy in the form of Bukharin and Stalin's "Socialism in one Country".

Like Brest Litovsk, socialism in one country was dictated by pragmatism rather than ideological sentiment. In both cases Russia had been so weakened politically and economically that she had to devote all her resources to internal reconstruction, leaving virtually nothing to pay for the defence of the nation, let alone an expansionist revolutionary policy as favoured by the Trotskyites. This was the logic of the Stalin-Bukharin faction. After they had defeated the leftists they studiously avoided helping communist movements abroad to overthrow their governments. For example, the Chinese communists were repeatedly advised by Moscow to ally with rather than fight Chiang Kai Shek's Kuomintang (KMT). This policy was dictated by the Kremlin's interests rather than by any keen consideration of events and possibilities in China, where the result of the policy was a massacre of communists by the KMT.

By 1929/30 Stalin was concentrating his nation's energies on industrialisation and collectivisation. At this critical stage any hostility provoked by Soviet adventurism abroad could have been harnessed to popular resentment within the USSR to bring down Stalin's regime. Throughout the 1930s the policy of retrenchment continued. Even with the rise of fascism in continental Europe, committed to the destruction of Bolshevism, local communists were encouraged by Moscow to cooperate with the bourgeois liberal and socialist parties in so-called "popular fronts". Stalin was more concerned that Russia should avoid attack by an alliance of centre and fascist parties than in promoting communism as a viable alternative to both fascism and liberalism in Germany and elsewhere.

The peak of this policy of retrenchment was the infamous Molotov–Ribbentrop pact of 1939. Germany's expansionist aims in the East were bought off by Stalin allowing the Nazis to take over half of Poland. As an added bonus to Moscow, Soviet troops took over the eastern half of that country.

The dilemma for the Kremlin in the period 1939–41 was whether to seek to join hands with the democracies of the West against fascism or whether to deal with the Nazis separately from those democracies and thus run the risk of attack from a liberal–fascist coalition. Both were forms of retrenchment. In practice the former alternative was not open. The leaders of Britain, France and the USA feared Stalin every bit as much, if not more, than they feared Hitler. Stalin thus had to deal with the fascist threat alone. He chose to do so in a way that angered the democracies but at a time at which a liberal–fascist alliance was unlikely.

It is not clear how long Stalin and Molotov expected the Nazi–Soviet pact to last. Russia had been rearming for several years before 1939 and stepped up its programme thereafter. Yet Stalin personally seems to have been thrown into a state of shock by the German invasion of the USSR in June 1941. Whatever the feelings of Soviet leaders, Russia was not prepared for war; the Nazis marched thousands of miles to the gates of Moscow within six months, leaving the Red Army scattered and in disarray.

The Soviets now found natural allies in Britain and the USA. Once again, as in the 1930s, retrenchment became a matter of necessity for the Kremlin. The wartime alliance saw closer cooperation between East and West than at any time before or since. In spite of the natural distrust of ideological enemies, the Soviets accepted American help under the Lend–Lease agreement and in turn kept German men and resources committed on the Eastern front when they could have been used to cross the Channel.

Towards the end of 1943 more formal coordination of the allied war effort became a reality with the Teheran conference. Stalin, Roosevelt and Churchill discussed the timing of the Normandy landings and a new Soviet offensive in the East. The Soviet Union's possible entry into war with Japan was also considered. Even more significantly for post-war politics the agenda covered the formation of the United Nations and the possibilities for peace after the defeat of fascism.

In February and July 1945 the leaders met again at Yalta and then Potsdam, reaching agreement on several vital issues. The Soviets, having dragged their feet at a previous meeting at Dumbarton Oaks in 1944, agreed at Yalta to cooperate in the setting up of the UN. Stalin also declared war on Japan. The West in turn agreed to accept the new Polish boundaries which registered the Soviet gains of 1939. In return Stalin promised free elections in Poland and accepted non-communist exiles into new governments in Poland and Yugoslavia. Yalta, however, marked the peak of cooperation. By the end of the Potsdam meeting only Stalin remained of the "big three"; Truman and Attlee proved more wary of making deals with the Generalissimo than had Roosevelt and Churchill.

This was one reason why arguments ranged in later years as to what was actually agreed in these meetings. "Free" elections and "democracy" meant different things in East and West. Within the USSR these arguments showed that there were factions who favoured revolution rather than retrenchment in the post-war situation. In wartime they sought to push Stalin into firmer backing for partisan movements in Poland, Yugoslavia and elsewhere and attacked the allies for their reluctance to open a second front in Western Europe to ease the burden on Russia in the East. In the West similarly one leader or faction took a different view of Soviet intentions to another.

After the victory had been won the USSR found her armies in effect in control of most of central Europe. To the revolutionaries (or "insurrectionists" as McCagg calls them) this presented a golden opportunity to spread communism to these nations. Even in countries where there were no Red Army troops the lead in fighting the fascists had been taken by local partisans sympathetic to communist ideas. In Greece, Albania, Yugoslavia, Iran and China there was an opportunity to expand communist influence in the world by "exporting revolution".

As if to strengthen the insurrectionists' case the main argument against them in the 1920s, that of Russia's weakness and vulnerability, no longer applied in 1945. After the war Russia had probably the largest and perhaps the strongest army in the world, a modern air force and a well-equipped navy. Surely now, if ever, was the time to spread the influence of her ideology.

To the moderates, however, retrenchment was still the best course in 1945. They saw the USSR's inbuilt weakness. The victory had been bought at enormous cost. As in the 1920s Russia had to rebuild her economy with a depleted population and little outside help. Was this the time, the moderates must have argued, to embark on foreign adventures? How too would the population who had made such sacrifices for four years to make the defeat of fascism possible, react to more years of high defence spending and economic deprivation? It cannot be forgotten that several parts of the Soviet Union experienced a severe famine in 1946 and that the economy of the West of the USSR had been largely destroyed in the war.

The main issue in Soviet foreign policy in Stalin's last decade was, therefore, the same one that ran through Soviet history until 1945 – revolution or retrenchment. In the countries under Red Army occupation, it was a question of whether the troops should gradually be withdrawn or whether they should be used to help establish pro-Soviet regimes in the capitals of Central Europe. Associated with this was the question of German reunification. Some wanted the eastern sector established as a separate state; others foresaw the reuniting of the country under the auspices of the United Nations. In the countries where partisan movements were strong the insurrectionists wanted the Kremlin to back them with all means at their disposal.

The moderates feared hostile Western reaction to any such extension of Soviet influence. They favoured a continuation of the wartime alliance with the West. The USSR would exert influence in, but not control, the East of Europe; the Americans and British would retain their hold over Western Europe and their colonies. To the moderates the activities of the Greek and Chinese communist insurgents seemed something of an embarrassment. They preferred to maintain the *status quo* with Soviet influence dominant only in those areas agreed at Yalta and Potsdam.

Foreign policy is not made in isolation. The actions and opinions of other states affected the options open to Soviet policy-makers. Most obviously the West's attitude towards Moscow changed in the aftermath of the war. Arguments continue to rage over whether it was East or West that was responsible for the "Cold War" that was in full swing by 1947. The fact is that some factions on both sides were in favour of it and others against it. In addition the delicate balance established amongst the Great Powers in 1945 was upset not simply by their leaders but also by the activities of politicians of all persuasion in countries like Iran and Korea. For example, Moscow's foreign policy in the 1940s was undoubtedly influenced by local communists. The arguments within Cominform (The International Communist "Information" Agency) that culminated in the expulsion of Tito's Yugoslavia were linked with events outside the USSR's borders and, to some extent, outside her control.

The main areas of concern for Soviet foreign policy-makers in the post-war decade were Europe and South-East Asia. Not until

Khrushchev's championing of Nasser's regime in Egypt did the Kremlin pay much attention to the African continent; neither was Latin America a central part of Soviet foreign strategy at this time; again it was Khrushchev and his alliance with Castro's Cuba that broke this pattern, several years after Stalin's death.

THE FORMATION AND IMPLEMENTATION OF FOREIGN POLICY, 1945–53

The foreign policy of the USSR is perhaps the best documented aspect of the post-war decade. Much has been written about the Cold War, the communist takeovers in Eastern Europe, the Berlin Blockade and the Korean War.[1] Most authors on the subject seem to agree that the USSR began the post-war era on a cautious note. Opportunities to extend communist influence in Greece, Iran and Austria were not taken up by Moscow in 1946 and 1947.

In Eastern Europe popular-front governments were allowed to continue in power. The situation worsened in the latter year as President Truman proclaimed his distrust of Russian strategy. At the same time the "hands off" policy favoured in Greece gave way to one of "communising" the states of Eastern Europe. Yugoslavia and Albania had gone communist without much help from the Kremlin; China was to follow the same path in 1948. In Bulgaria, Czechoslovakia, Hungary, Romania, East Germany and North Korea communist regimes were installed in 1947 and 1948.

Thereafter the Cold War hostility worsened. The Russians sought to solve the German problem by blockading Berlin in 1948. The West responded with a massive airlift and the formation of NATO in 1949. In June 1950 the North Koreans crossed the 38th parallel and set in motion a chain of events that led to Korean and Chinese communists fighting UN troops (sent under the strongest Soviet protest). Meanwhile in Eastern Europe the Kremlin's agents were supervising the removal of independent-minded communists from the leaderships of Eastern Europe as they pushed forward the development of Soviet-style regimes in these countries. They failed in Yugoslavia but succeeded elsewhere. After long negotiations the Korean war was ended only after

Stalin's death, which also brought to a halt the purges in Eastern Europe.

This chain of events was interpreted for many years in the West as part of a unified and consistent Soviet strategy aimed at world domination. The caution and popular frontism of 1945–46 was, according to this view, simply a case of Stalin biding his time whilst he prepared for the expansion into Eastern Europe, China and Korea. Since the 1960s, however, a revisionist point of view has emerged, attributing more responsibility for the Cold War to American mistrust of the Russians as epitomised by the Truman Doctrine. On this view, Stalin communised Eastern Europe and sanctioned the Korean adventure only because he saw these as the only way to secure the safety of the USSR and its allies against attack from the West. Furthermore Stalin himself seems to have felt that in 1945 and 1946 at least he had done no more than had been agreed at Yalta. He had not backed the Greek communists because Greece was in the agreed Western "sphere of influence". He had backed the Czech Party because that nation lay within the Soviet sphere.

Whatever the rights and wrongs of the situation, taken to extremes, both these points of view miss an essential feature of Soviet policy. Neither the Kremlin nor the world communist movement was united. The USSR reacted to events according to the views of those dominant in the Politburo and Cominform at the time. The Berlin Blockade and Korea may have been supported by different groupings than those who backed the coalitionism in Eastern Europe in 1945 and 1946 and allowed genuinely free elections in Czechoslovakia and Hungary.

The Kremlin also had to contend with the problems of implementing their foreign policy. Communists in foreign countries were not above putting their own gloss on the Kremlin's policy statements. The Chinese, for example, carried on their struggle with Chiang Kai Shek with little or no encouragement from Moscow. Their takeover certainly cannot simply be seen as part of a united world-wide communist strategy.

In order to understand more clearly the way in which Soviet foreign policy was made at this time we shall look in more detail at the areas of greatest concern to Soviet policy-makers: Eastern Europe and South East Asia and the Far East.

Eastern Europe

Within four years of the cessation of hostilities most of Eastern Europe was dominated by communist governments embarking on Stalinist policies at home and abroad. The speed at which this process occurred have led many to suppose that these "revolutions" were part of a carefully orchestrated plan carried out by a united leadership in the Kremlin. Seton-Watson, for example,[2] argues that the communist takeovers took place in three phases. In the first phase genuine coalitions of communist and other moderate left parties were the order of the day. In Czechoslovakia a "People's Front" government was established under the socialist Benes in March 1945. In the same month a "National Democratic Front" was established to rule Romania. In East Germany and Poland socialist parties were allowed to operate freely and participate in government. Only in Albania and Yugoslavia, where local partisans rather than Soviet troops had defeated the Germans, were fully communist regimes established at this early stage. Although other parties were encouraged to participate in government, and in several cases (such as Czechoslovakia and Hungary) provided the nation's leader, communists usually controlled the ministries of the Interior (and thus the police) and those in charge of information and agriculture (to preside over land reform).

According to Seton-Watson the communists used these positions to outmanoeuvre their opponents and to move into the second phase, which he calls "bogus coalition". In this stage other parties were allowed to exist but were driven out of government into opposition and harassed. In some nations such as East Germany, Hungary and Poland, the moderate socialist parties were combined with the communists to form a United Workers Party. Police power and the threat of the Soviet army were used to coerce other politicians into accepting and participating in Communist dominance.

This led to the third phase, that of the "monolithic block". Although other parties continued their formal existence, they became no more than puppets of the communists. Parties such as this exist to the present day in Poland, East Germany and elsewhere. They have no real power. Once communist domination had been achieved and all open opposition suppressed, the new regimes embarked on Stalinist policies of collectivisation and

industrialisation based on heavy industry, as well as the strengthening of a police state. As an example of the latter many
prominent East European communists, of whose loyalty Moscow
was unsure, were put on trial and executed in the late 1940s and
early 1950s: Slansky in Czechoslovakia, Rajk in Hungary, Kostov
in Bulgaria and Xoxe in Albania were all put to death. Only Tito
in Yugoslavia with his own army of partisans was able to resist the
Kremlin's pressures to conform. The men *he* arrested were the
Kremlin's agents rather than local communists who had not
been trained in Moscow.

As Seton-Watson notes, these phases did not occur in all the
countries concerned and their timing varied where they did take
place. Czechoslovakia, for example, avoided the stage of bogus
coalition altogether, moving straight from the first stage to the
third in February 1948. It is interesting to note, however, that
there were no Soviet troops in Czechoslovakia at the time. One
must not underestimate the genuine popularity of the Czech
communists who had won 40 per cent of the vote in pre-war
elections and 114 of the 300 parliamentary seats in May 1946. The
Red Army was a more significant potential threat in countries like
Poland which had strong anti-communist and anti-Russian
feelings than in communist-inclined Czechoslovakia or pro-
Russian Bulgaria.

Nevertheless, the way in which Hungary, Bulgaria, East
Germany, Poland, and Czechoslovakia moved in the same
political direction within a year or two of each other does suggest a
campaign coordinated and planned from Moscow. The agency
for carrying out this plan could well have been Cominform, the
establishment of which in the autumn of 1947 marked the end of
Popular Frontism in Eastern Europe. The old Communist
International, the Comintern, had been abolished in 1943 as a
gesture of goodwill to the allies to show that the Kremlin was not
trying to subvert their governments. Its revival in the form of an
Information Bureau was taken in the West as a sign that such
subversion had once again become an admitted part of Soviet
policy.

There can be little doubt that a majority in the Kremlin
favoured the communisation of Eastern Europe in 1947 and 1948.
However, it is not so clear that such unanimity existed in 1945 and
1946. It has been argued[3] that the second and third phases
outlined above were not a logical outcome of the basic philosophy

of the first phase but marked a distinct change of policy. The very fact that genuine coalitions ("Popular Fronts") were actually encouraged by Moscow in these countries in 1945 and 1946 suggests that Stalin and his colleagues may have been content to establish more moderate regimes in Prague, Budapest and the other capitals, provided only that such governments were not likely to allow their territory to be used as bases for attacking the USSR. Communist involvement in coalitions could have been sufficient to satisfy Soviet security needs. The fact that the Comintern was not revived until 1947 might imply that friendly rather than puppet regimes were all that Moscow wanted in Eastern Europe until the tide turned in 1947.

There could be several reasons for such a change in policy: firstly the American attitude seems to have hardened in the winter of 1946/47; secondly the factions in the Politburo favouring a more insurrectionist approach came more to the fore at the same time; thirdly the communists of these Eastern European states themselves were not always content to remain (sometimes junior) partners in coalitions and intrigued within their own countries and inside Cominform for a more militant stance aimed at outright power. We shall examine each of these arguments in turn and find that all three have some validity. As the US stance hardened, so the insurrectionist case became stronger in the Kremlin and in Cominform. Personal rivalries also played a part in this process: Zhdanov's ascendancy yielded a brand of revolutionary zeal that backed local communists' initiatives. After his death Beria used his secret police connections to stifle such initiatives. Later in 1951 Stalin sought to reduce Beria's power by purging some of his agents in Eastern Europe. The Kremlin was no more united on foreign affairs than in any other policy sphere. Even amongst those favouring full communist take-overs from 1947, some wanted regimes totally loyal to Moscow, whereas others favoured a greater tolerance of the national aspirations and difference of Czechs, Hungarians and so on.

Stalin himself certainly appeared resentful of what he saw as a change in American attitudes after the war. In an interview in May 1947 he said "when Roosevelt and I met we did not call each other such names. I am neither a sectarian nor a propagandist. I am a man of business."[4] He saw in President Truman a doctrinaire anti-communist who equated negotiation with the USSR with appeasement of the Nazis.

The Generalissimo had understood the spirit of Yalta and Potsdam to be one of post-war cooperation rather than antagonism. He had agreed to participate in the UN and to hold elections in East European states. In return he presumably expected to be allowed to manipulate the political scene in the Soviet sphere of influence sufficiently to make the zone neutral if not pro-Soviet. Russia had, after all, been attacked from the West three times in thirty years and Stalin and his colleagues surely felt justified in taking precautions against a recurrence. If Britain and France were allowed to keep their colonies why should Russia not hold sway over East and Central Europe? The promised free elections were actually held in Czechoslovakia and Hungary at national level and in other states at provincial level. Non-communist parties were allowed to operate relatively freely and were encouraged to participate in government if they were left of centre. The Politburo must have felt in 1946 that it was upholding both the letter and the spirit of the secret agreements of 1945.

Much had, however, changed in the West since Yalta. Truman and Attlee had come to power and from different ideological standpoints expressed distrust of Soviet motives. The defeated Winston Churchill, a man with whom Stalin had felt he could negotiate, had also reverted to his pre-war hostility to Bolshevism. His "Iron Curtain" speech in Missouri in 1946 showed how differently West and East interpreted the Yalta and Potsdam agreements. The West wanted nothing less than full liberal democracy in Eastern Europe; the Kremlin felt it could never go that far in countries like Poland and Romania where there were so few communists.

It was in the first half of 1947 that the American President launched the twin prongs of his anti-Soviet offensive: the Truman Doctrine and Marshall Plan. They were designed to combat a perceived Soviet aim of dominating war-ravaged Europe. The Truman Doctrine, a programme of economic and military aid to governments threatened with communist takeovers, was first put to Congress in March 1947. The real origins of the Cold War are seen by many as in the conference of foreign ministers in Moscow which broke up without agreement on 24 April. In June General Marshall announced his plan for economic aid to facilitate recovery in European countries. Even at this stage the Soviets did not reject it outright. Indeed the communist-led Czech government accepted Marshall aid, only to withdraw their acceptance a few days later under Soviet pressure. The initial acceptance had, however, not been to spite the USSR but because the Czechs saw it as something the Soviets would agree to as a logical extension of the wartime Lend–Lease programme.

The firm commitment to communisation came only after the Truman Doctrine and Marshall Aid had been announced. Cominform was set up in October 1947. "People's Republics", dominated by communist parties, were established in Romania and Czechoslovakia in the winter of 1947/48 to be followed over the next eighteen months by the other East European states. Truman's suspicions of the Russians were of course based on his and his advisers' views of Soviet interference in 1946 in states like Romania, Poland and Greece. The crucial issue in apportioning blame for starting the Cold War is whether the Soviets would have been content with popular front governments in Eastern Europe or whether they would have carried on to establish full communist regimes not only in the popular front states but also in countries like Greece, Austria, Finland and Turkey. Such historical "ifs" are unanswerable. Changing US attitudes, in particular, however, did lend weight to the arguments of the insurrectionists in the Soviet Politburo.

To show how the balance of opinion changed within the Politburo and within Cominform not just in 1947 but at other times, one must point to the inconsistencies in Soviet foreign policy. Varying policies in different places at different times show a constant struggle for authority amongst those senior officials who made Soviet foreign policy. Foremost amongst those men was Stalin himself. He kept far more closely in touch with foreign policy than with the domestic scene. The Politburo in his last decade saw a constant battle between men like Zhdanov, Malenkov, Beria, Molotov, Kaganovich and Mikoyan for Stalin's ear. The Generalissimo's ideas on foreign relations were not especially rigid; he could be moved by events and people to ignore pleas for help from the Greek and Chinese communists, whilst at other times sanctioning communist takeover in Czechoslovakia or seeking the overthrow of Tito's regime in Yugoslavia. He was also very aware of the need to prevent any one group of his lieutenants becoming too powerful. When he thought Beria or Zhdanov – or, for that matter, Tito – was becoming too strong he would set about undermining the man's power base by removing his lesser supporters and promoting his rivals.

There were foreign policy disputes within the Politburo even before the end of the war. In the winter of 1944/45 the Council of People's Commissars had set up a committee, chaired by Malenkov, to supervise the exacting of reparations from the occupied zones of Germany. Senior officials who later emigrated reported[5] that Zhdanov and Voznesensky attacked Malenkov's conduct of this task. His men were simply dismantling whatever plant and equipment they could find, with little regard for what German industry needed to survive, and shipping it back to the Soviet Union.The GOKO set up a commission headed by Mikoyan to investigate the problem. He recommended that the policy of dismantling be stopped and that German industrial plant be left *in situ* but exploited to produce goods badly needed in the USSR. This, Mikoyan would have argued, would be less wasteful; the cost of stripping down, transporting and then reassembling heavy machinery is enormous. It also did more harm to the German economy than utilising the equipment in Germany.

Kaganovich and Beria defended Malenkov, for both had a clear departmental interest in so doing. Kaganovich was at the time Minister for Building Materials and wanted advanced German machinery for his ministry's plants; similarly Beria wanted resources for the NKVD's vast economic empire based on slave labour in the prison camps. In spite of their protests Mikoyan's recommendations were accepted. Stalin was persuaded by Zhdanov that the establishment of Soviet–German joint stock companies would help the cause of the German communists in their country far more than the crude dismantling process which offered Germany nothing.

Interestingly enough the dismantling policy was continued in Manchuria. In spite of China's having a much stronger communist movement than Germany in 1945, Stalin and his colleagues had no scruples about ravaging China's industrial heartland only four years before Mao came to power. As we shall see in the next section, Soviet policy towards the Far East was rarely consistent with that towards Eastern Europe. Reparations were also exacted from Hungary, Bulgaria and Romania. As Deutscher points out this was an odd policy if Stalin intended to communise these countries in any case.[6]

As far as the Eastern zone of Germany was concerned the Soviet leadership changed its policy in 1945 because the Zhdanov insurrectionist faction based on the party managed to defeat the

Malenkov–Beria "Statist" faction in the battle for Stalin's favour. Even so there is some indication that the GOKO's policy was not implemented by the state machine quite as quickly as intended. A detailed study of the Soviet occupation of East Germany estimates that on average 50 or 60 per cent of the zone's 1936 industrial capacity in most major sectors had been dismantled by the end of 1946.[7] It is difficult to see how this could have been achieved unless the process carried on through much of 1945 and 1946. Many of the largest factories left in Germany's eastern zone were transferred to the control of Soviet enterprises in December 1945, but the dismantling process seems to have continued on a reduced scale.[8]

This reparations argument provides a very good example of how foreign policy was made, with struggling factories seeking to determine both Politburo policy and the way in which it was implemented. The Malenkov–Beria faction seemed to have little interest in the future of Germany, being mainly concerned with the potential benefit to the USSR. Zhdanov and his followers, on the other hand, were as early as 1944/45 aware of the possibilities for prompting communist takeovers in the capitals of Eastern Europe.

In the light of Zhdanov's insurrectionism it seems strange that the period 1945/46 (when it is usually assumed that he was the most influential figure in the Politburo, apart from Stalin) should be characterised by coalitionist policies. Popular fronts or united workers' parties were the order of the day in the states under Soviet control rather than pure communist regimes. Stalin himself probably saw in this policy a logical continuation of his pre-war tactics of building bridges with moderate socialists to present a united front to the fascists. It is possible, however, that Zhdanov saw the policy in a different way, as a means of infiltrating the socialist parties and thus of paving the way for communist takeovers. McCagg argues that Stalin gave way to the demands of the insurrectionists in his own leadership and in Eastern Europe and sanctioned the takeovers of 1947 and 1948 only to put himself in a position where he could isolate and defeat the Zhdanov faction.[9] Zhdanov was losing power before his death in 1948. After his demise most of his supporters were removed and a number of insurrectionists in Eastern European parties suffered a similar fate. The hardening of Soviet foreign policy in 1947 may be attributed to the pressure of the insurrectionists.

Stalin may have bowed to this pressure partly in order to reassert his own control over fellow communists at home and abroad.

The coalition of 1945/46 was on Stalin's part, at least, a genuine attempt to create friendly but not puppet regimes in the nations liberated by the Red Army. Competitive elections were held at national or local level in most countries. Their results were regarded even in the West as free and fair; only fascist-inclined parties were prohibited. Moderate parties were allowed to hold sway if they were popular. For example, the SDP, the German Socialist Party, was clearly the most important party in the Soviet zone in 1945/46.[10] Even after the SDP's merger with the communists to form the Socialist Unity Party (SED), the minority liberal and Christian Democrat Parties were encouraged to provide ministers for the provincial governments as late as October 1946. In Hungary elections in November 1945 resulted in a majority for the smallholders' party. Although Communist ministers were in the new government, Rakosi's men did not take control for another three years.

Neither were the policies of many of these governments overly communist until after 1947. For example, the German land reform of 1945/46 redistributed only a portion of the landlords' estates and gave the land into the private ownership of small-holders. Nationalisation of the land and collective farming on the Soviet model were not introduced until the end of the decade. There is no obvious reason why the Soviets should have tolerated moderate governments and policies in the first two post-war years, unless at this time dominant feelings in the leadership saw this policy as continuing for some time to come, in accordance with the Yalta and Potsdam agreements.

The argument that it was Stalin's intention all along fully to communise Eastern Europe and flout the spirit of Yalta and Potsdam also tends to ignore the facts that some countries did not go communist, because the Soviets never tried to impose their system, and that other countries did so without much help or encouragement from Moscow. Amongst the states of Central and Eastern Europe occupied by Soviet troops it could be argued that Austria was allowed to remain free because there was so little support for the communists who won only 5 per cent of the vote in post-war elections. However, the lack of a strong communist following did not prevent either Romania or Hungary falling under the Soviet yoke. Greece and Finland both had strong communist movements and at one time had Soviet troops on their soil yet the Kremlin made no move to communise either state. Soviet assistance to the Greeks in their civil war with the monarchists from 1946 to 1949 was reluctant and ineffective. In Finland communists and their sympathisers were leading lights in the coalition government but Moscow made no attempt to remove or infiltrate their opponents. As long as Helsinki remained friendly the Kremlin seemed happy not to intervene. Furthermore the communists had controlled the vital Ministry of Information; yet the normal pattern of communisation did not occur in Finland. Furthermore the situation in Iran with Soviet troops on hand, separatist movements by Kurds and Azerbaidzhanis and growing anti-Western sentiment, was ripe for revolution. Yet under Western pressure, Stalin agreed to withdraw his troops in May 1946. It must not be forgotten that Western Europe also saw communists involved in coalitions in Italy, France and Belgium as part of the coalitionist policies. These coalitions broke up in 1947 under pressure from the West rather than the East, and without inducing any positive Soviet response.

Further evidence of the inconsistency of post-war Soviet foreign policy can be found in Stalin's reluctance to help the communists in China and Vietnam to secure their ends. A fuller discussion of this will be left to the next section. However, it does show that the Politburo's aim was not uniformly and consistently to expand communist influence wherever possible at whatever cost. No doubt some of the Politburo wanted this, others were more concerned with the security of Russia's western frontiers, and still others were more concerned with their own departmental interests rather than national ones. We have already seen how departmental concerns influenced the reparations question. In addition Zhdanov's insurrectionism was linked to the party revival he was masterminding within the USSR. To him the communist parties under the supervision of the Russian party were the vehicles for exporting the Soviet system. Although Zhdanov had no formal responsibility for foreign affairs, he seems to have exercised enormous influence in this sphere until 1947 within the Secretariat. The effect of this was to make the Secretariat more of a force in foreign policy-making at the expense of the Foreign Ministry. The foreign minister until 1945 was Molotov; he was succeeded in that year by A. Ya Vyshinsky.

Neither wielded as much authority in this sphere after the war as had Molotov before it.

The other leading Politburo member with a strong departmental interest in foreign policy was Beria who, at least until 1951, had overall responsibility for the security police run by the MVD and the MGB. Officials and agents of both organisations were deeply involved in the takeovers of 1947 and 1948 in Eastern Europe. Whilst Zhdanov was working with local parties to foment revolution in Prague and Budapest, Beria was using Soviet control over the Interior ministries in those capitals to infiltrate and control the forces of law and order. These agents later played a key role in plotting the removal of leading East European communists such as Rajk in Hungary, Koster in Bulgaria and Gomulka in Poland. This first wave of purges in Eastern Europe in 1949/50 was aimed at communists who had not been trained in Moscow and so whose loyalty to the Kremlin was open to doubt, Beria appears to have persuaded Stalin that many of the insurrectionists, whom Zdhanov had backed until 1947, had to be removed, especially after the split with Tito revealed the dangerous possibility of communist regimes independent of Moscow ruling Eastern Europe. To Stalin that possibility was worse than the domination of these countries by non-communist but friendly governments.

The other body that one would expect to influence foreign policy was the military. Yet Stalin was jealous of the power and influence Zhukov and his fellow soldiers had acquired in the war. In 1944/45 he lost no time in eroding their power demoting Zhukov and eventually appointing Bulganin, a politician, to keep the military in check as his Minister of the Armed Forces.

The changes in Soviet foreign policy in Stalin's last decade were in many cases directly related to personnel changes in the leadership. For example Malenkov's removal from the Secretariat in 1946[11] marks a perceptible shift towards party-led insurrectionism as illustrated by the sudden merger of socialist and communist parties in East Germany, the communist victory in the Czech elections and the declaration of a communist-led front government in Bulgaria. Zhdanov favoured communist party takeovers in Eastern Europe and elsewhere with substantial scope given to the initiative of local party members.[12] To that extent he was a more genuine internationalist than Malenkov or Beria. They saw takeovers in Eastern Europe as a means of securing

Russia's defences. Their policies aimed at establishing local communist regimes with no room for local initiative.

The balance of power between the Zhdanov and Malenkov factions tilted in favour of the latter over the expulsion of Yugoslavia from the Cominform in 1948. When Cominform was founded in September 1947 Malenkov and Zhdanov were appointed joint Soviet representatives. Zhdanov's authority in foreign affairs was already being compromised. Indeed the very establishment of a new international communist organisation can be seen as a device to impose uniformity on the movement, a policy associated with Malenkov and Beria. Zhdanov emphasised the agency's role in coordination and propaganda rather than dictation. At the same time Stalin could have attributed the West's increasingly hostile stance as partly due to Zhdanov's encouraging the insurrectionists abroad. As McCagg argues Stalin was caught between Western pressure and that of insurrectionists within his own and other parties. Malenkov and Beria offered a possible way out of this dilemma. Stalin could promote them to challenge Zhdanov's authority whilst encouraging takeovers in Eastern Europe only to purge and Stalinise the new regimes within a year or two of their coming to power.

This tactic is obvious in the split with Tito. Stalin's first attacks on the Yugoslavs in January and February 1948 were over Tito's plans for a communist "Balkan Federation" uniting his country with Bulgaria (and, by implication, Greece).[13] Yet Stalin himself had planted this idea in Tito's mind! Tito incurred Stalin's displeasure not because he advocated reformist policies; at this time he was amongst the most loyal of communists. His crime lay in having his own power base in the partisan army that had brought him to power and thus not being dependent on Moscow. The whole Cominform dispute appears to have been engineered by Stalin with the help of Malenkov, Beria and Suslov to remove Tito, Djilas and their colleagues and replace them with a leadership more dependent on Moscow. As Stalin is reported to have said after the Yugoslavs had been expelled from Cominform: "I will shake my little finger and Tito will disappear."

In the first six months of 1948 M.A. Suslov and P.A. Yudin both played a key role in fomenting discord with the Yugoslavs. Both were allies of the Malenkov–Beria faction. Suslov along with Zhdanov and Malenkov attended the meeting of Cominform in June 1948 at which Tito was expelled. By July Malenkov had been restored to his post in the Secretariat. After Zdhanov's death in August Suslov took over his responsibilities for foreign policy and ideology within the Secretariat. The removal of other Zhdanov allies such as Voznesensky, Kuznetsov and Popov followed over the following eighteen months. In addition foreign minister Molotov lost his position in early 1949. Although he remained a member of the Politburo he had not lost his place as Stalin's deputy and heir apparent by this time. Molotov was not a member of Zdhanov's group but had allied with them on a number of issues. He was probably more associated with the popular front policies of the 1930s and 1945/46. They were outdated by 1948/49 and Molotov's eclipse became inevitable.

The ascendancy of Malenkov and Beria was marked by a drive to sort out Eastern Europe: to install thoroughly pro-Stalin regimes there and to solve the Berlin issue once and for all. East European communists who had not been trained in Moscow were rooted out and, in some cases, put on public trial and executed in the manner of the Soviet show trials of the 1930s. These operations carried the stamp of Stalin and of Beria's police network. At the same time the Soviet model of a centrally planned economy based on heavy industry and collectivisation in agriculture was imposed on most Eastern Europe regimes that had moved cautiously on land reform in 1946, as had the Soviet occupation administration in East Germany, now opted for full and rapid collectivisation, as put into practice in the USSR in 1929/30. This Stalinisation of Eastern Europe marked the peak of Malenkov and Beria's power.

The Berlin question had long been a thorn in this strategy. As long as that city in the middle of the Soviet zone remained, partly in Allied hands, East Germany could not be Stalinised and made a secure part of the USSR's defences. In 1947 the Russians refused to accept the new currency introduced in West Germany. They feared Berlin would become a spearhead for the penetration of Western influences into the East. In March 1948 the Soviets began to impose restrictions on rail traffic from the West to Berlin. At Yalta Stalin had agreed to allow access to the city via fixed road and rail corridors through the Eastern zone. In June (in the same month as Tito's expulsion from Cominform) all road traffic from the West to Berlin was halted. The timing and nature of the policy clearly associates it with the Malenkov-Beria faction. The policy failed because of a massive Western airlift to help the stricken

West Berliners. Secret East–West talks began in February 1949 and the Soviets agreed to lift the blockade in May. From that time the existing division of Germany was established. The Federal Republic was founded in the same month and the GDR some six months later. To this extent the Germany problem was resolved and the westerly limits of Soviet defences accepted by the Americans and British.

By the winter of 1949/50 Stalin was becoming concerned at the extent of Malenkov and Beria's authority in both foreign and domestic matters. The Generalissimo began a series of moves aimed at reducing that influence. These continued until Stalin's death. The famous "Doctor's Plot" of 1952 was probably a prelude to an attempt to remove either Malenkov or Beria or both. The manoeuvrings began late in 1949 when Khrushchev was brought to Moscow to balance Malenkov's power in the Secretariat. In the following year one of Khrushchev's protégés and a former Zhdanovite, S.D. Ignatev replaced Beria's man, Avakumov as Minister of State Security. This direct attack at the heart of Beria's power base was followed by purges of his supporters in Georgia in the Mingrelian Affair of 1951. The relevance of this attack for foreign affairs lies in the purging of some of Beria's agents in Eastern Europe at the same time. The MGB was directly in charge of security operations abroad. Ignatev organised the arrest of several of Beria's men in Prague early in 1951, of whom it is alleged Rudolf Slansky was one.[14] Slansky was publicly tried in 1952, perhaps as a warning to other Beria supporters. Nevertheless both Malenkov and Beria seem to have weathered the storm until Stalin's death. Their influence on foreign policy must therefore have remained significant during the most acute East–West confrontation during the Korean War of 1950–53.

As in other policy spheres leadership quarrels over foreign affairs were reflected in scholarly controversies. For example the Varga affair had obvious implications for foreign policy. In 1945 he published preliminary chapters for a new book in which he stressed the possibility of capitalist countries making a peaceful transition to socialism. This implied that there was no great need to foment revolution abroad and that energies could be devoted to fighting the fascist enemy. In 1945 this was a perfectly respectable statement.[15] By 1947, however, as the coalitionist line became less tenable, Varga and his Institute of World Economy and World Politics came under attack within the Institute of Economics.

Varga, however, survived and in fact never fully recanted his views. Perhaps he was fortunate in as much as the arguments carried on into 1951 and 1952 by which time coalitionism and peaceful coexistence with the West were once again becoming respectable notions.

No such reprieve awaited G.F. Aleksandrov, a senior official in the secretariat's Agitprop department, who in 1945 expressed a similar belief in the possibility of communism coming about through a variety of patterns of development. In 1947 Aleksandrov was removed from the secretariat. His "liberalism" would appear to have placed him in opposition to the insurrectionists. Yet in some ways it was the Zhdanov group that was more tolerant of "different roads to socialism" and the Malenkov-Beria axis that sought to impose a standard pattern on Eastern Europe. The policy positions of both groups must be understood in their full complexity in order to understand the changes that took place between 1947 and 1949.

South-East Asia

As in Europe Soviet policy towards South-East Asia in the post-war decade has all the hallmarks of expansionism, not only in 1947, but continuously up to Stalin's death. In 1945 there were no communist regimes in this area. In 1945 Ho Chi Minh set up a provisional government in Hanoi that finally defeated the French Colonialists in 1954. The communists were in full control of North Korea by the end of 1947. Two years later the People's Republic of China was proclaimed in Peking. Eight months later the North Koreans launched an offensive against the American-controlled South and the Korean war began. This war was the closest the two great powers came to armed combat. US troops in the guise of a United Nations Force fought firstly Korean guerrillas and later Chinese soldiers armed with Soviet weapons.

Paradoxically at least two authors on this subject, McCagg and Shulman, see 1949–53 as a time of consolidation ("blocism" as McCagg calls it) rather than expansionism in Russian policy. Stalin's efforts were aimed at securing complete control over his bloc rather than expanding its frontiers. Shulman argues that from 1949 there were strong moves within the Soviet leadership to pursue a more conciliatory policy towards the West, backing the peace movement in Western nations and protecting such dissident liberal voices as Varga's.[16] Certainly Stalin had more to lose than to gain from escalating the Cold War. He was acutely aware that the Americans had nuclear weapons. In spite of a crash development programme supervised by Beria the Soviet atom bomb was not usable even in 1953. Furthermore the conventional forces of the USSR had been run down from $11\frac{1}{2}$ million at the end of the war to only three million in 1947. They were built up again to $5\frac{1}{2}$ million at the time of the Korean war, but there were grave doubts as to whether the Soviet economy could withstand another war. The USA had the atom bomb and had suffered no direct losses in the world war. She would surely have outgunned Russia in any conflict and Stalin and his colleagues were well aware of this.

The Soviet expansionism in South-East Asia can be explained by Russian reactions to American pressure and by the insurrectionism of Asian communists as well as by a Soviet desire to retain her hold over her own sphere of influence.

The communist insurgency in Vietnam dates from 1941. The Japanese invaders then threw out many of the French colonial administrators. When the Japanese in turn surrendered to the Allies in August 1945 there was little organised opposition to Ho Chi Minh's Viet Minh guerrillas. A Provisional government was set up in Hanoi in the autumn of 1945. However, the French were not willing to give up the colony without a fight. They regrouped their forces and embarked on a campaign that lasted until the battle of Dien Bien Phu in 1954 after which the State of North Vietnam was recognised as independent. Throughout this successful guerrilla action the Russians did little or nothing to help the local communists. Stalin's Politburo were far more interested in Europe than Asia. Their concern was primarily the USSR's Western defences. Vietnam was of little strategic significance to the USSR, being separated from the Soviet Union by 2000 miles of Chinese territory. Neither was the post-war Politburo very keen on supporting revolutionary movements that had their own bases of support and so did not have to rely on Moscow.

Korea was different from Vietnam in both respects. It occupies a key position for the USSR's eastern defences against Japan and its revolution owed less to the activity of local guerrillas and more to the presence of Soviet troops on Korean soil. An ex-colony of Japan, Korea had been deemed unsuitable for independence by both the great powers at Yalta in 1945. It was thus put under the protection of the USSR and the USA with the Red Army occupying the Northern Zone above the 38th Parallel and the US Army the South. As in Germany the two sides failed to agree on the future of the country. In effect North Korea became a separate state under the Communist leader Kim Il Sung in 1947. Stalin's leadership communised North Korea as they did Eastern Europe and at the same time. This Asian policy had the same motives behind it as had the takeovers in Europe. The end of coalitionism in Korea was, however, also hastened by an American-inspired UN vote to hold elections for a National Assembly in a United Korea. In the spring of 1948 the Soviets refused to allow a UN supervisory commission over the 38th Parallel. Separate elections were held in North and South. Those in the North were, of course, managed to ensure a communist victory, although the strength of Kim Il Sung's regime was shown by the fact that all Soviet troops were withdrawn in the autumn of 1948.

The establishment of North Korea was the first time that the West used the UN as a vehicle to attack the USSR. They followed this up by persuading the UN assembly to elect Tito's Yugoslavia to the Security Council in 1949. In the same year the UN refused to admit the new communist regime in China. A year later Korean and Chinese communists found themselves fighting UN troops. The USSR boycotted the UN. Stalin had in 1945 accepted the organisation as a forum for superpower agreement (in the Security Council). The Soviets were willing to work within a UN framework, but not if the West mobilised the smaller nations against her. Stalin had seen the UN as a means of keeping these smaller nations under the control of the superpowers, not as a way of arbitrating between them.

The Chinese civil war erupted again as soon as the Japanese surrendered. Mao's communists and Chiang Kai Shek's Kuomintang had been fighting each other periodically since the 1920s. In fact on more than one occasion before the war it had only been Moscow's insistence on its policy of popular frontism that had forced Mao into alliance with the KMT (usually with adverse results). The Kremlin was not at all happy about the civil war breaking out in 1945. Stalin wanted a peaceful China as a bulwark against possible Japanese aggression on Russia's eastern borders. Right up until 1949 he seemed to give little for Mao's chances of achieving this by fighting against the KMT. Perhaps Stalin was more concerned that Mao would seize power without Soviet help and create a new Yugoslavia on the USSR's borders. China was like Korea to the Soviet authorities in terms of its strategic significance, but like Vietnam in terms of the independence and military strength of its communist movement.

When Mao proclaimed the People's Republic of China in Peking in October 1949 Moscow could no longer ignore his movement. After several months of negotiation a Sino–Soviet friendship treaty was signed. The USSR promised enormous economic and military aid to China including the return of resources taken from Soviet-occupied parts of China in 1945.

Only four months after the treaty was signed North Koreans crossed the 38th Parallel and invaded the South. Their rapid advance was halted by the deployment of UN troops under the command of the American General MacArthur. The 16-nation combined force pushed the communists back northwards. Peking threatened armed intervention if the UN troops crossed the border into North Korea. When they crossed the Yahi river and did so, Chinese soldiers were sent to help the North Koreans and reestablish the status quo. The war dragged on until 1953 when an armistice registered a new border not very different from the old one on the 38th Parallel.

Naturally enough in the climate of the time the Korean adventure was regarded in the West as part of a Soviet attempt to take over South-East Asia. If, however, the attack was master-minded from Moscow then it is possible that Malenkov or Stalin thought that the Americans had lost interest in Korea when they withdrew their forces in 1948. As had already been explained Korea is of great strategic importance to the USSR and became even more so when the potentially independent Chinese communists came to power.

It is by no means certain that the Kremlin did prompt or even sanction the attack. In view of the Politburo's generally cautious line at this time it is feasible that the North Koreans themselves took the initiative with or without Peking's backing. They were equipped with Soviet arms but so were all the countries that had been communised in 1947/48.

In summary the Korean war may have been intended by all parties in Cominform as a *Korean* conflict not involving the superpowers. Few politicians in Moscow managed to understand why the Americans should react so strongly to events in countries so far from their own soil. Peking and Pyong Yang had similar problems of comprehension. There is no evidence of serious disagreement within the Soviet Politburo or Cominform over the Korean escapade. Yet it does not fit in with the general trend of Soviet foreign policy under Stalin and Malenkov. The most likely explanation for this paradox is that the initiative came from the Koreans themselves, but was not considered by Moscow to be important enough to prevent.

CONCLUSIONS

Soviet foreign policy during Stalin's last decade was not a consistent strategy. The popular frontism that characterised the first two post-war years seems to have been a genuine attempt to establish loyal but not necessarily communist regimes in Eastern Europe and Korea. This policy was closely associated with Stalin himself. This coalitionism was, however, open to different interpretations. Zhdanov and his followers saw in it a means of communist infiltration of other Front parties and so a covert path to insurrectionism. This view was shared by a number of local communists who wished to follow the examples of Tito in Yugoslavia and Hoxha in Albania and set up communist systems. It was also an image common amongst Western leaders.

This alliance of Zhdanovites and local communists was not strong enough in 1946 to overcome Stalin's opposition to insurrectionism. The hardening of American attitudes and the failure to reach agreements over the make-up of the post-war world early in 1947 forced Stalin's hand. Popular frontism was no longer a viable policy under these circumstances. In 1947 and early 1948 Stalin gave way to the insurrectionists' demands, although only in countries within the agreed Soviet sphere of influence. The Generalissimo kept hoping to the last for a change in Western attitudes.

Stalin was well aware that by acceding to insurrectionist policies he was giving too much power to the Zhdanov party revivalist faction. He had promoted this faction since 1944 to balance the influence of the Malenkov–Beria state faction and Zhukov's military in domestic affairs. By 1947 Zhdanov had become too powerful, a challenge to Stalin himself. Stalin's response was to accept Zhdanov's foreign policy but remove his supporters at home and abroad. Within the USSR he promoted the Malenkov and Beria faction once again. They supervised the removal of most of Zhdanov's allies in the Politburo and the Secretariat in 1948 and 1949 and promoted their own men.

Malenkov and Beria's ascendancy in foreign policy was marked by the consolidation of Soviet control over the recently communised states. Beria's police agents manipulated the removal of insurrectionist elements in foreign communist parties. Moscow ordered rapid collectivisation and expansion of heavy industry in the satellite states.

Even then there were enormous variations in the implementation of these policies. Collectivisation ranged from 20 per cent to nearly 80 per cent in other states. Executions were common in the Czech and Bulgarian purges. In Poland and the GDR there were no political executions at this time. There were limits to Moscow's control over policy in Eastern Europe.

As Malenkov and Beria became too powerful in turn, Stalin began to manoeuvre against them, removing Beria's allies in the secret police at home and abroad. Soviet foreign policy from 1949 gradually began to adopt a more coalitionist attitude. Particularly after the failure of the Korean escapade, Moscow seemed again to be looking towards accommodation with the West rather than confrontation. As in 1946 such a policy meant different things to different people. Khrushchev, as his post-Stalin record shows, favoured peaceful competition between capitalism and communism. Beria, on the other hand, seemed to view peaceful coexistence as a cover for secret police operations that would eventually bring more states into the communist camp.

Foreign policy was a field in which Stalin personally was extremely interested. Even so, he could not decide matters on his own; he had to take some account of the views of the rest of the Politburo and of the other members of Cominform. If he did not, he put his own authority in danger and ran the risk of his directives being reinterpreted in a way that did not suit him. It was his arch enemy Harry Truman who said in June 1948, "I like old Joe. He's a decent fellow but he's a prisoner of the Politburo."[17] It is true that Stalin sometimes sought to give this impression to facilitate a later change of mind but, to a degree, it would appear to be an accurate picture. He was the most important figure in Soviet foreign policy at the time but by no means the only one of any significance.

6 Cultural Policy

INTRODUCTION

Cultural values are a matter that does not concern governments very much in the West. The Soviet regime however has always taken a keen interest in what is written, said and broadcast in their country. On the one hand this reflects a long Russian tradition of preoccupation with the arts. The casual visitor to the USSR even today cannot help being struck by the breadth of interest in literature and the cinema. The communists have strengthened the link between the writer and film-maker and the political system. As we shall see, even music and such remote academic studies as linguistics came to the centre of political attention during Stalin's last decade.

The term "cultural policy", as used here, really covers two distinct fields: the fine arts and political propaganda. They are grouped together because it has never been easy to distinguish the two in the Soviet Union. The 1917 revolution gave birth to a mass of cultural experimentation, much of it voluntarily serving the new regime. The emerging film industry was harnessed to spread the message of communism throughout the length and breadth of the USSR. Such famous directors as Eisenstein and Pudovkin lent their services to this cause. In poetry the verses of Mayakovsky often had a deep political significance. Soviet writers of prose sought to emulate the socialist realism of Maxim Gorky.

The immediate post-revolutionary period saw a blossoming of talent based on the freedoms allowed by the new regime. It also witnessed the expansion of the Soviet propaganda machine and its use of the arts to spread its message. Full political control over culture did not however become a reality until the 1930s. Satirists like Ilf and Petrov as well as the (later disgraced) Zoshchenko flourished in Soviet literature in the 1920s.

It was towards the end of that decade, as industrialisation and collectivisation got under way, that Stalin's regime made a determined effort to harness Russian culture in the service of the party and the government. This was in part a voluntary movement, led by the enthusiasts of "proletarian culture". As in so many other cases, however, it was used by Stalin and his cronies to establish firm guidelines for Soviet culture. The writer and musician were to write in service of the party. They could not be apolitical; they must positively develop regime-supportive values. Furthermore they had to follow themes that were readily approachable for the ordinary citizen. The excessive experimentation and modernism so prevalent in the 1920s were discouraged in the following decade.

The main organs of this control over the arts were the unions and the secretariat of the party. Any writer, composer or film director who did not conform could find himself excluded from the relevant union, as a result of which he or she could not work. Literary censorship was (and is) formally the province of a *state* agency (in the 1940s the State Committee on the Arts), but in practice the party department in charge of propaganda and culture has always determined the guidelines within which it should operate.

The other and main responsibility of the secretariat department for Agitation and Propaganda was to control the flow of political information to the masses. It was from here that Soviet propaganda, which in the 1930s increasingly resembled Orwell's "doublespeak", was masterminded. Embarrassing or inconvenient facts, such as the extent of the purges of the 1930s, were not mentioned. "Positive" aspects of the regime such as economic achievement and the speeches of leaders were glorified. This reached ludicrous proportions in the Cult of Personality that surrounded Stalin in the 1930s. A short, fat and slightly deformed man with an unfortunate Georgian accent, Stalin was transformed by the propaganda machine into a huge, handsome charismatic figure, the father of a nation. His flattering portraits were posted everywhere like royalty. His public appearances were strictly rationed and accorded massive publicity whenever they took place. His role in history, especially in the revolution was grossly exaggerated. In the infamous "Short Course" party history, he even corrected the text himself to emphasise his own importance to future generations who were to learn from the text. Towns and cities were named after Stalin. His closeness to Lenin was exaggerated as the posthumous cult of the leader of the revolution was built up. The personalities and the role in history of Stalin's defeated enemies like Trotsky and Bukharin were defamed. This creation of enemies "from within" was a device calculated to unite Soviet citizens behind Stalin's leadership. At the same time Stalin's supporters were allowed to develop their "mini cults" in the areas they controlled, or from whence they had come; the city of Perm in Siberia was renamed Molotov; the name of Beria came to be lauded in his native Georgia at only one step below that of Stalin.

As the 1930s progressed central direction of the arts and academia tightened and the cult spread wider and wider. The war, however, wrought profound changes in both culture and propaganda in a more liberal direction. Values that had been proscribed until 1941 suddenly received the stamp of official approval in both culture and propaganda. The Russian heritage became as important as, if not more so than, the communist tradition. Articles began to appear in the press in praise of great Tsarist Generals like Suvorov who had defeated Napoleon's armies. Even some of the old monarchs themselves, like Ivan the Terrible and Peter the Great, came in for some positive reassessment. Now medals were named after Suvorov and others; and signs of inequality of rank, such as epaulettes and saluting officers were reintroduced in the Red Army. *Russian* nationalism was the new spirit to be fostered, not communist internationalism, not even *Soviet* patriotism. As adjuncts to this the Orthodox Church, the hated foe of Lenin's propagandists, was allowed something of a revival. Similarly Slavophilism with its emphasis on the common ethnic roots of many Soviet citizens, was permitted a resurgence. The reason for the nationalist revival was obvious. It was a means of uniting the nation against the German invader. Stalin and his wartime propaganda chief Shcherbakov must have considered nationalism a more potent force for national unity than socialism. Only ten years after the horrors of collectivisation and five after the Great Purge this is not very surprising. People who would not fight to save the Bolsheviks would do so to save Mother Russia. Indeed the episode has become known in the USSR as the Great Patriotic (or Fatherland) War.

During the war years propaganda was aimed more at equating the regime with popular values than seeking to change those values in accordance with the dictates of the leadership. The propagandists stopped attacking mythical Trotskyite enemies and concentrated on the very real foe on Soviet soil. The violent anti-German sentiments expressed in, for example, the works of Ilya Ehrenburg, still find an echo in the USSR today.

In the arts, patriotism and other new values provided a new alternative for the writer and the composer, but they did not release him from his duty to the state. He was expected to disseminate these values as he had the pre-war communist and party values of socialist realism. Perhaps a more potent force for liberalism in wartime came from new contacts with the West. After years of isolation Soviet cities now found themselves in contact with Hollywood films, Western novels and Western goods sent under the lend-lease agreement. As soldiers or as officials many Soviets gained their first opportunity of seeing life in other countries at first hand. In many ways the propaganda machine had to moderate its criticisms of the capitalist way of life as it was encouraging Russians to fight a common enemy alongside the capitalists.

In summary the war led to a liberalisation of Soviet propaganda and cultural controls that led many to foresee a much brighter future after the victory had been won. Just as some hoped for an easing of the collective farm system in 1945, so others looked forward to a blossoming freedom in the arts. The writer Vsevolod Vyshnevsky spoke to the Society for External Cultural Relations in the following terms in the summer of 1944.[1]

When the war is over, life will become very pleasant. A great literature will be produced as a result of our experiences. There will be much coming and going, and a lot of contacts with the West. Everybody will be allowed to read whatever he likes. There will be exchanges of students, and foreign travel for Soviet citizens will be made easy.

As early as 1944 the opposite point of view was already being expressed. Party men in the Zhdanov mould were alarmed at what they saw as the laxity of the wartime years. They could accept its necessity when the USSR was under siege in 1941 and 1942, but as the tide of the war turned in 1943 they began to worry about the future. At the 9th Plenum of the Writers' Union in February 1944 official attacks were made on authors who ignored their political responsibilities. The two authors singled out for special attack were Mikhail Zoshchenko and Konstantin Fedin.[2] Both were accused of apoliticism. Zoshchenko in his *Before Sunrise* had shown an unhealthy preoccupation with his own feelings rather than with the tide of history and social development. Fedin's memoir on Gorky was overly concerned with the narrow life of the literary world and relationships within it.

Fedin also attacked, by implication, the notion of *"partiinost"* in literature, that novels should propagate appropriate social values in a positive way and glorify the role of institutions like the party. *Pravda*, the organ of the party's Central Committee, took great exception to this. As early as 1944 the party revival was closely associated with calls to reactivate political control over the arts. The revivalists also appear to have disliked Shcherbakov's popularisation of propaganda. They wanted a return to a disciplined agitprop machine propagating good communist values like *Soviet* patriotism, hard work, the leading role of the party and the importance of Marxism Leninism rather than the Russian nationalism, religion and bourgeois western influences that had been allowed in 1941–43.

By the end of the war this issue was still unresolved. Throughout 1944 and 1945, although there was some attempt to clamp down on extremes of liberalism, both lines continued to be tolerated. The works of apolitical and individualistic writers like Zoshchenko continued to be published in spite of the attacks on them. Indeed he was awarded a medal early in 1946 as a reward for his "valiant work in the Great Patriotic War".[3]

The main issue in cultural policy after the war was thus whether to continue the wartime thaw or to extend the party revival into a reassertion of the pre-war controls over the arts and propaganda. In examining post-war policy we shall look first of all at the cultural scene and then consider the politics of agitprop, included in which is a discussion of some of the academic debates on philosophy and linguistics that were surprisingly closely linked to the party leadership.

POST-WAR CULTURAL POLICY: FORMATION AND IMPLEMENTATION

The arts and political control

Post-war policy in this sphere can be divided into four phases. The first of these up to August 1946 was a continuation of the dualism of the last years of the war. Although the party in particular attacked wartime laxity and apoliticism it continued to flourish and on occasion receive official blessing.

By August 1946 however Zhdanov was strong enough within the Secretariat and Politburo to embark on the attack on artistic and intellectual life that became known as the "Zhdanovshchina". The change of policy was marked by the 1946 decree of the Central Committee attacking two Leningrad literary journals. Attacks on the cinema, composers and others followed. In their wake economists, philosophers and others also came under attack for the lack of political purpose in their works. Other charges levelled in all these spheres were that the role and reputation of the party was being undervalued and that there was an overpraising of everything western and consequent underrating of Soviet achievements.

During Zhdanov's ascendancy, there were virtually no imprisonments or executions. This was an ideological purge in which examples were made of famous people. It was not a witch hunt of the type that followed in the next phase. After Zhdanov's death under the influence of Malenkov and Beria there began an attack on the influence of "rootless cosmopolitans" in Soviet life. This campaign was only partly anti-semitic; its roots were in attacks on those whose attitudes were still too favourable to the West and on those in the union republics who were toying with "bourgeois nationalism". It was also used as a cover for attacks on some of Zhdanov's former supporters. This campaign was considerably more violent than the Zhdanovshchina proper.

As Stalin began to erode Beria's power in the early 1950s so there began to emerge signs of a thaw in the strict controls over culture that had grown up in the previous two phases. Liberals were appointed to certain key posts in the literary establishment and a genuine attempt was made to lift Soviet drama out of the rut in which it had fallen over the previous three or four years. By 1952 the "thaw" that became so famous in the Khrushchev era (partly due to Ehrenburg's novel of the same title) had already begun.

The beginnings of the "Zhdanovshchina" in August 1946 were clearly associated with Zhdanov himself and opposed by other factions within the party and state. On the 14th of that month a central committee decree appeared attacking two Leningrad literary journals *Zvezda* and *Leningrad* for publishing "apolitical" and "ideologically harmful" works of authors such as Zoshchenko and Akhmatova. Leningrad was Zhdanov's power base and his fiefdom. Such an attack was either organised by him or against him. A few days after the decree had been issued Zhdanov himself addressed a meeting of Leningrad writers at which he criticised Zoshchenko's "Adventures of a Monkey". To the Central Committee secretary this escapist tale of an animal's adventures in war-ravaged Russia represented "Soviet people as so many idlers and moral monsters and as generally stupid and primitive" and "oozed anti-Soviet poison".[4]

Zoshchenko's mild satire might just be construed as "anti-ideological" and "disorienting to the nation's youth"[5] but Akhmatova's love poems seemed hardly to merit such criticism. But to Zhdanov and his supporters they were full of pessimism and self-obsession. She too was guilty of the sins of apoliticism and enticing the minds of the nation's youth away from more "positive" themes such as the glory of work and the achievements of Soviet citizens and (of course!) their party and its leadership and their Marxist creed.

The immediate results of the decree were the reorganisation of *Zvezda* and of its editorial board. *Leningrad* was closed down completely. Both Akhmatova and Zoshchenko were subjected to further attacks by the Zhdanovite writer Fadeev who was first secretary of the writers' union. Both the miscreant authors were expelled from the union and so lost their livelihood. However neither was arrested. The Zhdanovshchina itself was an attack on people and ideas that stopped short of physical sanctions. Imprisonment and execution were not Zhdanov's tools at this time.

The singling out of two journalists and two writers did not mean that the attack was confined to them. The decree was a signal to the entire Soviet literary establishment that apoliticism and self-indulgence would no longer be tolerated. The first post-war era of the two lines was at an end. Writers were now expected to act once again as the servants of the party and the state. They were to promote values that would help to rebuild the economy and reinforce ideological orthodoxy. They had to glorify all things Soviet and especially the party. Manifestations of foreign influence or individualism were now frowned upon. There was no question of avoiding rather than opposing these dictates. Authors had to show a positive approach to Soviet life in their works or else they would not be published and the writer could lose his living.

There are a few signs of opposition to Zhdanov at this stage. Although he had a clear majority for his policies within the Secretariat and Politburo, the newspaper *Pravda* did not publish the decree until a week after the Central Committee had approved it. It seems that even within Zhdanov's own ideology section of the Secretariat, which supervised the running of *Pravda*, there were still some who did not share his views.

In general, however, the campaign against apoliticism was run by the party Secretariat. It was a key part of the Party revival. As such it aimed to induce a return in official values from wartime laxity to what Hahn calls "principled communism".[6] Just as Zhdanov and his allies wanted good communists to take power in Eastern Europe and elsewhere and rule through their parties with a key role assigned to their agitprop departments, so they wanted the same type to cooperate with the Soviet party in its bid to control Soviet literature. The organs that Zhdanov used to implement his campaign were the Writers' Union, the agitprop department of the Central Committee which was responsible for the decree), and the latter's journals *Kultura I Zhizn* ("Culture and Life") and *Partiinaya Zhizn* ("Party Life").

The Zhdanovshchina was soon extended to the cinema. A decree of September 1946 attacked apoliticism in films, notably in "The Great Life" a film about the Donbass mines, which (amongst other errors) ignored the decisive role of the party in the reconstruction of the area. Like Zoshchenko's story it showed Soviet citizens as far removed from the hard-working sober ideal favoured by the Central Committee's agitprop department. Even such great names as Pudovkin and Eisenstein came under attack. The latter was criticised for Part 2 of his film "Ivan the Terrible". It is well known that the history of that Tsar and his "*Oprichnini*"

(Tsar Ivan the Terrible's personal guard) formed a close parallel to Stalin's autocracy and the role of the secret police. Now it appeared that Eisenstein's conception made out both Tsar and followers to be too vulgar and imprincipled. Perhaps Zhdanov had in mind currying favour with Stalin, who had personally told the actor playing Ivan of his sympathies for the bloody Tsar. It seems unlikely, however, that his criticisms should aim at defending Beria's secret police. Zhdanov probably saw his own party revivalists as the group loyal to the leader defending him against his enemies, as did the *Oprichnini* for Ivan. Although neither Eisenstein nor Pudovkin was dismissed or arrested, the criticisms had a severe effect on the Soviet film industry in general and on Eisenstein's health in particular.[7]

The final sphere of culture to fall victims to Zhdanov's ideological requirements was music. To the Westerner it is difficult to see how classical music could have deep political implications. Yet Zhdanov managed to level charges of apoliticism and modernism against such world-renowned figures as Sergei Prokofiev and Dmitri Shostakovich. They and other composers had apparently failed to celebrate the 30th anniversary of the revolution in November 1947 with the required fervour. In February 1948 the Central Committee decreed that a variety of Soviet composers were guilty of "formalism". By this Zhdanov meant the sort of non-melodic avant garde music that appealed only to a restricted audience. Music, declared the agitprop department, should be tuneful enough for the masses to understand and should celebrate Soviet achievements in a readily approachable fashion.

The vehicles for Zhdanov's attack were once again the agitprop section of the Secretariat and the Composers' Union. Yet the attack on music in the winter of 1947/48 differed in vital aspects from the earlier stages of the Zhdanovshchina. By this time Zhdanov's influence was already on the wane as the international situation worsened. The attempt to establish party control over music was an effort on his part to stem the tide against his party revivalist faction. He failed to do so. The campaign in music was less important than that in literature or cinema (media where the political message is more direct). In spite of this, composers felt freer to oppose Zhdanov than had writers or film directors. The composer Shebalin refused to recant, and Prokofiev's "self-criticism" was not satisfactory to the revivalists. One leading composer simply refused to attend a meeting called by Zhdanov to condemn formalism.[8]

That tide was turning against Zhdanov by the winter of 1947/48 is shown by the public criticisms of Fadeev in December 1947. Fadeev, Zhdanov's man at the heart of the Writers' Union had received a Stalin prize for his novel about the Komsomol *The Young Guard*. Only a year later it was criticised by *Pravda* and *Culture and Life* for playing down the role of the Party.[9] His work thus appears to have fallen foul of his own theses of 1946. With hindsight it seems more likely that this was a warning to Fadeev couched in terms of Zhdanovite rhetoric, but masterminded by Malenkov and Suslov, becoming even more important in the Secretariat. Fadeev heeded the warning, confessed his errors and agreed to rewrite the work. He retained his post as first secretary of the Writers' Union and assisted in the "anti-cosmopolitan" campaigns of 1950/51.

By the time of Zhdanov's death in October 1948 Malenkov and Beria were at least as powerful as the revivalists. His demise tipped the balance decisively in their favour in literature as elsewhere. The result was not a liberalisation but an increasingly violent and less principled crackdown on both liberal artists and their opponents, Zhdanov's supporters. The initial reaction to Zhdanovism was in a liberal direction but this was soon turned into a campaign against the liberals and their bourgeois Western or cosmopolitan leanings.

The field in which this stage of the Soviet cultural battle took place was drama. In March 1948 (six months before Zhdanov's death) the Council of Ministers cut the level of grants to Soviet theatres on the grounds that they were not getting good enough audiences. Plays had become lifeless and uninteresting under Zhdanov's reign and people would not go to watch them. A series of articles critical of the state of Soviet drama followed. These developed into attacks on the no-conflict theory, the idea that Soviet characters in plays should not really argue with each other because they had the same interests at heart.[10]

Within two months of Zhdanov's death the campaign had been turned against the critics themselves. With Zhdanov out of the way Malenkov, Beria and Suslov no longer had to feign liberalism to attack his hard line. They were now free to indulge their own even tougher policy. At a plenary session of the Writers' Union Fadeev attacked critics like Malyugin and Borshchagovskii for defaming Soviet dramatists. They were accused of attacking honest Soviet playrights rather than the real enemy, bourgeois Western culture. In taking this stand Fadeev was remaining true to his hard-line policies, although that entailed a move from the Zhdanov to the Malenkov–Beria faction.

Fadeev's words were given the highest official sanction on 28 January 1949 when Pravda published an editorial "On an Anti-Patriotic Group of Theatre Critics". They were accused of using abstract formalism as a cover for their anti-Soviet feelings. From here it was but a short step to the denunciations and public humiliations of the anti-cosmopolitan campaign. Theatre critics and others were accused in often very crude terms of being an organised anti-Soviet group. In a series of events reminiscent of the public self-criticisms and show trials of the 1930s all attempts at any kind of liberalism in Soviet literature were quashed. The campaign also took on a decidedly anti-semitic tone. To which other ethnic group could the term "rootless cosmopolitan" apply? Many but not all of the condemned critics were Jewish. In all probability Malenkov and Beria added in the anti-semitism to give more popular credence to their charges against their enemies. Under the guise of attacking the cosmopolitans they could remove not only liberals but also Zhdanov's former supporters in the agitprop section. Some of the latter, as well as a number of writers, suffered imprisonment or even execution at this time.

The development of the anti-cosmopolitan campaign coincided with a series of decrees on such famous party journals as *Krokodil Znamya* and *Ogonek*.[11] *Krokodil* was criticised for the weakness of its satire, but it was made clear that its target should be bourgeois culture and such "capitalist survivals" in the USSR as bureaucratic red tape. It was also accused of having a closed group of contributors. Its editor and several of his board were sacked. The board of *Ogonek* was similarly purged. These events in September and October 1948 presaged the attack on cosmopolitanism in theatre by several weeks. In January 1949 it was *Znaniya*'s turn. It was accused by the Central Committee of not having learnt the lessons of Zhdanov's August 1946 decree. Although the artistic quality of its articles was deplored, so was its ideological level. The Secretariat was not prepared to make any concessions to artistic freedom to produce more interesting contributions. In the words of the decree:

In the pages of the journal they should publish articles correctly and clearly showing life in its revolutionary development, revealing the new high quality of Soviet people – the builders of Communism. Led by the method of socialist realism, Soviet literateurs must more bravely bring to life and searingly underline everything new and communist and bravely fight those survivals that prevent the Soviet people moving forward.[12]

The language and spirit of Zhdanov was being used to attack both his enemies and his supporters. There is no evidence that Malenkov, Beria or Suslov disagreed with Zhdanov's cultural policies; they resented the man's power and influence; if anything they seem to have felt that his hard line was not hard enough. Zhdanov's men were removed from the editorial boards of the journals run by the agitprop department (*Ogonek*) and by *Pravda* (*Znaniya* and *Krokodil*).

A further manifestation of the new tough line came in July 1951 when *Pravda* attacked the Ukrainian poet V. Sosyura for his "bourgeois nationalism".[13] Patriotic feelings towards any of the union republics were equally as cosmopolitan as the anti-Soviet attitude that failed to denounce capitalistic culture.

However by this time a thaw was already appearing in this cultural freeze. Several writers have recently pointed to a liberalisation in Soviet literary policy from early in 1952.[14] It seems that the roots of this policy go back to the winter of 1949/50.[15] They coincide with various moves by Stalin to limit the growing power of the Malenkov–Beria axis. One of these moves was the promotion of Khrushchev to the leading circle. As his later decision to publish Solzhenitsyn's "*One Day in the Life of Ivan Denisorsch*" shows, Khrushchev could at times prove sympathetic to new and different trends in authorship. Another of Stalin's moves included the 1951 Mingrelian affair, a purge of many of Beria's supporters in his (and Stalin's) native Georgia. Charges of bourgeois nationalism were levelled at those purges.[16] It is thus possible that the attack on bourgeois nationalism in literature was not part of Malenkov's anti-cosmopolitan campaign, but part of Stalin's own campaign to erode Beria's influence. This would not have been the first time in Kremlin power struggles that the policy stance of the enemy has been used against him.

Beria of course survived Stalin's attempts to unseat him but he could no longer stem the tide in favour of cultural liberalisation. Slowly but surely the thaw which became the subject of popular commentary in 1954, began to gather momentum in Stalin's last three years.

As early as the summer of 1949 the agitprop department renewed its attack of the previous winter on Soviet drama. This time, however, besides the normal criticisms of undervaluing the party and Soviet people in general, the playwrights Sofronov and Kozhevnikov were criticised for poor artistic workmanship.[17] Even during the anti-cosmopolitan campaign moves were afoot to raise artistic standards in Soviet literature.

The journal that had published these plays was *Novy Mir*. In February 1950 its editor Konstantin Simonov was replaced by Aleksandr Tvardovsky, the same man who was to show his colours as a defender of anti-establishment writers under Khrushchev and Brezhnev. Both Simonov and Tvardovsky were well-known figures in the Soviet literary establishment and *Novy Mir* one of the most important literary journals. The change of editorship must have been an official signal of hope to the liberals. At about the same time *Ogonek* published a few poems by Akhmatova. Although not as radical as her earlier work, this was the first time she had been published since 1946 and presumably reflected her readmission to the Writers' Union.

In March 1950 *Pravda* launched a fierce assault on the critic Belik, whom they accused of resurrecting "the sectarian views of the RAPP-ists".[18] In fact Belik's review of a book on Soviet literature by A. Tarasenkov was quite conventional by the standards of 1949, making a RAPP-style demand for positivism and socialist realism. He equated the latter with obeying the party line and glorifying party organisations. Belik was singled out for attack in 1950, as a signal to others that the denunciations of the previous year would no longer be allowed to frustrate the development of Soviet writing. As the *Pravda* article said, "A socialist art cannot be created by outcries and blackjack [destructive – T.D.] criticism".[19] Party organs like *Pravda* combined with *Literaturnaya Gazeta*, run by the Writers' Union, to call a halt to the annihilation of opponents by unreasonable criticism that characterised 1949.

This did not, however, mark a new flowering of Soviet literature. Both author and critics were wary that the new line might change as quickly as the old one had done. The Secretariat, however, continued to issue signals that genuine improvements in literature were needed. In September 1951 a Central Committee Decree once again condemned *Krokodil* for the weakness of its satire. This provided a preview of the call for satire that accompanied the 1952 campaign to revitalise the written word in the USSR.

In the early months of 1952 criticism of the no-conflict theory in drama was resumed. Once again it was pointed out that the idea that there was no conflict in Soviet society or at least only a contrast of "good" with "better"[20] was the reason why so much Soviet drama was uninteresting. The plastic characters of the Zhdanov era and of 1949 should give way to people in situations and dilemmas nearer to real life. In July of the same year *Novy Mir* took a substantial step towards implementing this policy by publishing the works of Vasily Grossman and Valentin Ovechkin. Grossman's *For a Just Cause* took a positive Soviet theme – the Battle for Stalingrad – but allowed its characters to spend time on the sort of personal philosophising for which Akhmatova had been condemned in 1946. *Novy Mir*'s editors, including Tvardovsky and Tarasenkov, were forced to admit their error in publishing the first part of Grossman's novel, but only after a lengthy interlude. Grossman never recanted. In fact, as Frankel points out, criticisms of him continued *after* Stalin's death. This is a clear sign that the mainstay of the attack on the new liberalism was the Malenkov–Beria axis who came to the fore in the months after Stalin's death.[21]

Ovechkin's "Raion Routine" (*Raionnie Budni*) contained a portrait of a disinterested and remote party official in a rural area that flatly contradicted the model of 1946–9. Yet there was little if any strong criticism of his work. It is possible that he had backing from a high position for his views, possibly from Khrushchev, now Malenkov's main rival for the succession.

1952 can be seen as a year not simply of thaw, but of two lines, reminiscent of 1945. Liberal viewpoints were expressed but the hardliners had not given up. The Central Committee promulgated two decrees in 1952 attacking publishers for issuing collected editions of classic authors that were insufficiently politicised. In October, at the Party Congress, Malenkov sought to justify both political controls over literature and the sort of exaggerated image of the Soviet hero that permeated the works approved of by the hardliners.[22] By the time of Stalin's death the two lines were in open conflict; after it many (including Fadeev) feared a further clampdown. Within days of Stalin's demise Malenkov had united the Ministry of Higher Education with the State Committee for the Arts to form a new Ministry of Culture under his supporter P.K. Ponomarenko. Only in 1954 and 1955 did the full spirit of the thaw of 1952 really come to fruition. Even then some of the criticised works, including Grossman's novel, were never published again in their original form.

Agitprop: propaganda, political training and philosophy

In the terminology of Marxism–Leninism "propaganda" describes the process of enlightening the elite, the intellectual and political leaders of society. "Agitation" refers to the political education of the masses through such media as radio, daily newspapers and books. In the sphere of propaganda Soviet policy in the 1940s ebbed and flowed in a similar fashion to controls over culture. The last two years of the war had seen a revival of the party and of its role in propaganda. The energies of the agitprop section had been devoted in 1941–4 to agitation using such previously anti-Soviet values as Russian patriotism, religion and friendship with the West. In January 1945 Zhdanov returned from Leningrad to the Central Committee Secretariat in Moscow. The head of the agitprop department A.S. Shcberbakov did not appear in public after December 1944 and died in August 1945. Zhdanov took over his role and began to reassert both the importance of propaganda and the need for Marxist and Soviet values.

In September 1945 P. Fedoseev, editor-in-chief of the party's theoretical journal *Bol'shevik* published an article about Lenin's theory of imperialism. Soon afterwards a Central Committee decree attacked the former editors of the journal for their lack of attention to the basic tenets of Marxism–Leninism.[23] The editorial boards of several other agitprop journals were purged at the same time.

By 1946 Zhdanov was the unchallenged head of Agitprop. He established two new journals to preach the message of the party revival – the propagation of pure and principled Marxism, neither the laxity of wartime liberalism, nor the vulgar Marxism–Leninism of the pre-war purges. One journal, *Culture and Life* was aimed at the cultural establishment; the other *Party Life* was to spread the good word to the rank and file of the party in the provinces.

Typical of Zhdanov's attempts to enforce his views was the attack on G.F. Aleksandrov's *History of Western Philosophy*. The book, intended as a basic text for Soviet educational institutions, had been well received when it was published at the end of the war. In June 1947 Zhdanov accused its author of divorcing philosophy from everyday problems, the same apoliticism of which Akhmatova and Zoshchenko were guilty. Furthermore Aleksandrov had by implication placed Marxism in the stream of Western philosophy. By this and his failure to analyse any Russian philosophers (the book dealt only with the period up to 1848) Aleksandrov showed himself to be anti-Soviet in Zhdanov's eyes. Most seriously Aleksandrov had failed to point out that Marxism was distinguished from other Western philosophy by its scientific nature. The hapless author was removed from the Agitprop department. Zhdanov's influence was, however, already on the wane; Aleksandrov survived to head the Institute of Philosophy of the Academy of Sciences and be re-elected to the Central Committee in 1952.

As the international situation worsened, so Soviet agitation and propaganda acquired what Zhdanov would have called a more ·vulgar Marxist tone. Things foreign were generally frowned upon. In the second half of 1947 foreigners' movements were severely restricted within Russia by government order; there was a tight clampdown on information.

In academic life this period, which coincided with the rise of Malenkov, saw the advance of Lysenkoism. Lysenko and his genetic theories were not part of the Zhdanovshchina proper. Zhdanov and his son both seem to have sought to resist Stalin's attempts to promote Lysenko's theories and denounce the alternatives.[24] To them the idea that plants like humans could learn from their environment and so could be "brainwashed" into giving better yields may well have seemed like a parody of Marxism-Leninism.

Zhdanov's death in August 1948 left the field open for Lysenko and for Malenkov. Under the latter's direction the Agitprop section changed course. One of the more bizarre examples of the anti-cosmopolitanism-based-on-Marxist rhetoric of 1948/49 was the claim that Russians had invented such items as the electric light bulb and the telephone. This was part of the xenophobia and

Soviet patriotism in vogue at the time. Like Lysenko's theories these claims have since proved to have little validity. Under Malenkov their main use was to instill in people of all ranks a loyalty to the party and the state that did not depend on understanding complicated Marxist rhetoric. Once again agitation became more important than propaganda, although there was no sign of the Western liberal values of 1944. *Party Life* ceased publication. A Central Committee decree of November 1948 attacked the publishers of political posters for their lack of orientation towards such real life problems as strengthening Kolkhoz discipline, contrasting the USSR's peaceful aims with the West's aggression and celebrating the achievements of Soviet factories in fulfilling their plans.[25] Malenkov wanted Agitprop to agitate on behalf of the production and foreign ministries, not inculcate people in the spirit of Marxism–Leninism. In July 1949 he succeeded in removing Fedoseev, Iovchuk and other Zhdanov supporters from the Agitprop department.[26]

Another bizarre note was struck in 1951 by the appearance of Stalin's work on linguistics. Why such a specialised field of study should become the concern of one of the most powerful men in the world and dominate the Soviet press is hard to explain. It has been suggested that Stalin wanted to make his mark as a theoretician, as well as a man of action, before he died. Perhaps he was simply becoming senile. Whatever his reasons this and his *Economic Problems of Socialism in the USSR* were the only major public manifestations of his thinking between 1947 and 1952. Most of the pamphlet was an attack on Nicolai Marr who had devised the utility of comparative analysis in linguistics. Some saw in Stalin's message a sign that foreign influences and a more liberal approach to literature and propaganda might be tolerated.[27] However, Stalin still affirmed that if there was a future universal language it would be based on Russian, an idea that fits in with the anti-cosmopolitan absurdity of 1949. In practice the Agitprop department took the wise course of avoiding the issue as far as they could. They did not wish to offend Stalin, but they did not want his work to signal a new liberalism in propaganda or culture. There can be little doubt that if there was *any* political message in Stalin's book it was a veiled attack on the anti-cosmopolitanism of Malenkov and Beria. As its publication came at about the same time as the Mingrelian Affair, this could have been Stalin's intention.

In September 1951 the Central Committee published a decree on the new *Great Soviet Encyclopedia*. Its editors were condemned not for political errors but for having contributions written by little-known (but presumbaly "safe" authors) rather than well-respected figures in the field.[28] Like the origins of the thaw in literary policy, this was a muted call for higher standards (and thus a more liberal outlook) in academic life and propaganda. By 1951 Malenkov and Beria's dominance was being challenged. Yet it was only months after Stalin's death that their power was finally broken. March 1953 did not see a great change in Soviet agitation and propaganda or in policy towards the arts. That transition had already begun two or three years earlier.

CONCLUSIONS

Cultural policy in the post-war decade was above all the province of the party and its Secretariat's Agitprop department in particular. The State Committee on the Arts, directly subordinate to the Council of Ministers, often had to decide whether a new play should be performed or a new novel published. But it was on several occasions overruled by the Secretariat. To be accurate the committee made no attempt to rival the Agitprop department, it merely tried to interpret the Party's moods as accurately as it could. Inevitably at times it was caught out as the party line changed abruptly.

The Writers' and Composers' Unions were in a similarly subordinate position. They carried out the dictates of the party. Only when the party leadership was tolerating two lines could these unions find any freedom to express their own views. Men like Fadeev and Khrennikov (of the Composers' Union) were caught between political superiors demanding conformity and portions of their membership wanting more artistic licence. Only when the former allowed were the latter feelings satisfied and even then only to a limited degree.

The battle was then for control of the Agitprop department and of the Secretariat. Once he had ousted Shcberbakov in 1945 Zhdanov manoeuvred himself into a position of authority. Malenkov, his main rival, was transferred from the Secretariat. In

August 1946 the Zhdanovshchina began in earnest. Initially in 1947/48 Malenkov and Beria used the liberal tack as a means of tackling Zhdanov's power. As soon as he left the scene Malenkov was strong enough in the Secretariat and the Politburo to revert to his own version of the hardline. This became more ruthless and violent as the decade came to an end culminating in the vicious campaign against rootless cosmopolitans. By 1950, however, change was again in the air, masterminded by Stalin himself and possibly involving Khrushchev and others.

Stalin was not strong enough at the time simply to dismiss Malenkov and/or Beria. He had to manipulate policies and people to undermine their substantial power bases. The natural vehicle for undermining Malenkov's authority in the Secretariat was liberalism. Stalin himself was no more of a liberal than Malenkov had been earlier in 1948. He used liberals' policies to chip away at Malenkov's power bases. This explains why Stalin did not let the thaw of 1950–53 go too far; he thought it would get out of his control, with unacceptable consequences for the future. In any case Malenkov was too strong at this time to be completely unseated from the Secretariat. Perhaps Stalin did not want to do so; he may have been content to limit Malenkov's authority and detach him from Beria's influence.

Beria was arguably the man Stalin feared most, a fear that was echoed by many others in the Politburo who remembered the police purges of the Party leadership in the 1930s. Stalin's manoeuvres against Beria took a much harder line than those against Malenkov. The campaign against bourgeois nationalism in literature by its timing and content was almost certainly aimed at Beria.

˙The main conflicts within Stalin's leadership in cultural policy were, therefore, not between liberals and hard-liners, but between different sorts of Stalinists. Zhdanov and his supporters favoured enforcing a brand of Marxism–Leninism that was probably nearer to the intentions of the founders of the Soviet state than that of Malenkov and Beria. The latter's more opportunistic stance in cultural matters reflected a lack of concern with ideology. To Zhdanov ideas and beliefs were basic; to Malenkov they were just a means to the ends of economic achievement and keeping himself and the party in power.

Nevertheless liberalism did raise its head in the USSR several years before Stalin's death. That event did not mark a watershed in Soviet policy; the real change seems to have come after Beria's arrest and execution later in 1953. Even then there remained many in the Soviet literary and political establishment opposed to anything that did not positively expound the values of Soviet patriotism and hard work and the virtues of the Soviet system and the communist party.

7 Conclusion

POLITBURO POLITICS 1945–53

Stalin was not quite the dominant all-powerful leader in his last decade that the pure totalitarian view would suggest. His was the most powerful voice in the Politburo but he could not always overrule the majority view amongst his colleagues. In particular he had to resort to underhand manoeuvres over several years in his (unsuccessful) bid to limit the power of the Malenkov–Beria axis. Furthermore he did not make his policies in a vacuum. He had to listen to the advice and information brought to him by his Politburo members. They naturally struggled with each other for the Generalissimo's ear.

The limitations to Stalin's authority were thus twofold. On the one hand he had to rely on colleagues to keep him informed and carry out his orders. On the other hand his personal incapacity grew as the years passed. His advancing age allied to his disillusionment over American and British policies at the outbreak of the Cold War in 1947/48 kept him out of the limelight after that date. His only public appearance was a very brief one in 1952. He spent most of his time either in the Kremlin or at his country dacha. Increasingly his mind wandered from affairs of state. Which Western politician would concentrate his public energies on linguistics and economic theory at a time when the Korean war was reaching a critical phase and agricultural problems were rearing their ugly head?

Stalin was obviously not completely senile, nor was he addicted to alcohol or drugs (as has been suggested), at least not so much as to cloud his mind to the danger of Beria's power. The manoeuvrings at the 1952 Party Congress show that the old master still had his finger on the political pulse. He announced the creation of a new enlarged Politburo (renamed the Presidium) of *more* than 20 members. This gave Stalin the chance he wanted to pack the leadership with new younger men like S.D. Ignatev, M.Z. Saburov and L.I. Brezhnev, who had few links with Beria and Malenkov. In fact several (like Brezhnev) had strong career links with Beria's arch rival Khrushchev and were later promoted under his leadership. Yet neither Stalin nor Khrushchev was able to prevent the promotion of Malenkov and Beria supporters like M.A. Suslov and P.K. Ponomarenko (who had been demoted to a ministerial portfolio for the years 1950–2) – only one of the old Politburo was dropped – the already disgraced Andreev. Stalin could not remove Beria's supporters nor prevent the promotion of some of them. He had to resort, Khrushchev later revealed, to the subterfuge of creating a small governing body within the Presidium which had no formal or public status and so was more amenable to being bent to the dictator's will than the old Politburo.

Despite these limitations to his authority Stalin could still intervene decisively on some policy matters. For example his personal backing of the geneticist Lysenko seems to have guaranteed him immunity against other enemies in the Politburo. The Generalissimo's opposition to Khrushchev's plans to revitalise agriculture by giving the peasants themselves a better deal also appears to have been decisive. Yet on both these matters Stalin had the support of the Malenkov–Beria faction. It is not clear whether these two Politburo members allied with their leader as a matter of convenience or even vice versa. As Conquest says, personal power considerations and policy matters were very much intertwined in this period.[1]

All that can be said with certainty is that Stalin had to resort to the same intrigues, plots and arguments that his senior colleagues had to use. He could not command obedience from them in the manner of an absolute autocrat. This fact is well illustrated by two very disparate events. Firstly in 1947 Stalin had to bow to pressure from the Zhdanov faction in the Politburo and their allies in foreign communist parties to end the policy of popular frontier in Eastern Europe. Western attitudes helped to push Stalin into the insurrectionist camp, but his personal commitment to the idea of communist alliance with moderate socialists was shown by the Yalta and Potsdam agreements, by his remarks to Djilas in 1946[2] and by the fact that he seriously considered accepting the American offer of Marshall Aid in early 1947. Furthermore popular frontism was historically linked with his name from the days of "socialism in one country" to the anti-fascist blocs of the 1930s.

The second illustration of Stalin's use of intrigue rather than command was the Mingrelian Affair of 1951/52. In the winter of 1951 regional sub-units within the Georgian republic were reorganised so as to limit the power of the Georgian Party Secretary, K.N. Charkviani, a close ally of Beria. Within a few months Charkviani and the chairmen of the Georgian Soviet and the Council of Ministers had been removed, along with hundreds of other senior officials in the republic. Few were shot; most of them reappeared in April 1953 after Stalin's death, with Beria again ascendant. They were however condemned in Central Committee Resolutions for tolerating Georgian nationalism. At least four of those purged were of Mingrelian nationality, as was Beria himself. According to Khrushchev Stalin issued the Central Committee resolutions himself without clearing them with his colleagues. He did so not because he was an autocrat but because he could not risk Beria's being able to frustrate this move. Despite these events Beria survived until Stalin's death and was then strong enough to play a leading role in it until Khrushchev managed to arrest him six months later.

The main factions in the Politburo during the period 1945–53 centred on the younger leaders Zhdanov, Malenkov, Beria and Khrushchev rather than more senior figures like Andreev, Mikoyan, Kaganovich and Molotov. The last was effectively Stalin's deputy at the end of the war, but his star went into decline thereafter, although he remained in the Politburo. Mikoyan and Andreev suffered a similar eclipse, even, according to Khrushchev, being excluded from Politburo meetings on Stalin's orders. The leader would not have been able to exclude Malenkov or Zhdanov in this way.

Of the major figures in the Politburo in the 1940s Zhdanov was the most senior having joined it in 1935 and becoming a full member in 1939. He lost ground as a result of his involvement in the subsequently abortive Nazi–Soviet Pact. The party revival that had its origins in 1943 marked his return to favour. His fortunes were at their highest from the summer of 1946 until the next year. He gained control of the Secretariat and was widely regarded as Stalin's heir apparent. His revivalist and insurrectionist views held sway in culture and foreign policy respectively. On the agricultural front he backed Andreev's attempts to spread the revival onto the collective farms. In industry it was the economic voluntarists led by Voznesenskii who allied to the Zhdanov cause. Their imprint is laid on the 1946 Five Year Plan. Voznesenskii himself became a full member of the Politburo in February 1947.

Of the 1947 Politburo Zhdanov probably had the support on a number of issues of both Molotov and Mikoyan from amongst the old guard. Amongst the junior candidate members Bulganin and Kosygin may also have had some links with the revivalists[3] Khrushchev, who had joined the leadership in 1938 and headed the prestigious Ukrainian party organisation, was also something of a revivalist and certainly had no love for Beria and his police methods as later events were to show. In all Zhdanov had the full or partial support of six of the 11 full Politburo members and two of the three candidate members. The Secretariat early in 1947 consisted of Stalin, Zhdanov, A.A. Kuznetsov, G. M. Popov, and N.S. Patolichev. The last three all had strong ties with Zhdanov; Kuznetsov was shot after Zhdanov's death in the infamous Leningrad Affair. Patolichev survived in a junior position until he returned to the enlarged leadership of October 1952. Popov was demoted in 1949.

Zhdanov's power began to wane in 1947/48 with the appointment of first Suslov and then Malenkov to the Secretariat. They seem to have masterminded the split with Tito that would surely have presaged Zhdanov's removal if he had not died in August 1948. Malenkov and Beria then set about removing former Zhdanov supporters. In 1949 the Leningrad Affair revealed a so-called plot emanating in that city. In its wake many politicians were arrested and shot, the most famous being Voznesenskii, Rodionov and A.A. Kuznetsov. With these moves and Zhdanov's death the "statists" gained a working majority on the Politburo. With Mikoyan and Molotov having lost much of their influence Beria and Malenkov put themselves in a dominant position in the 1949 leadership. They could often bank on the support of Kaganovich, Voroshilov and Shvernik against the revivalists. The Secretariat by the end of 1949 was staffed by stalin, Malenkov, Suslov, P.K. Ponomarenko and Khrushchev. Only the latter's appointment in December 1949 prevented Malenkov's total dominance.

Under Malenkov Zhdanov's "principled" hard line became a more pragmatic set of policies. They were, if anything, less liberal and more violent than Zhdanov's but were justified more by reference to economic growth and state security than to Marxist rhetoric. Many more died and were arrested in 1949 and 1950 than in Zhdanov's heyday. This turn in policies was most marked in foreign affairs with the communisation of Eastern Europe and in culture with the campaign against cosmopolitans.

From 1950 Stalin with the help of Khrushchev sought to undermine the authority of the statists. In most policy spheres they allowed a flirtation with more liberal ideas like peaceful coexistence, more artistic licence and a better deal for the collective farms as a means to oppose Malenkov and Beria. As at other times policy positions could be adopted by Stalin as a means of attacking an individual's power. Khrushchev later was to prove that his relative liberalism was rather more genuine.

Stalin's attack on the statists was incomplete at the time of his death. His daughter recalls Beria's apparent glee at the Generalissimo's passing. This can be attributed to his feelings at the demise of his main opponent. Not long before his death Stalin had presided over the "Doctors' Plot", a fabricated case in which Kremlin doctors were convicted of attempting to murder senior Politburo members. There seems little doubt that Beria would have been implicated in this affair if Stalin's plans had run their full course. It is possible that Malenkov could have suffered the same fate, although without the backing of Beria's police connections his power would not have been as great a threat to Stalin.

This analysis of the factional politics of 1945–53 would not be complete without mention of the links between them and the lower organs of Soviet power. Each of the major figures in the Politburo had his supporters amongst the ranks of lesser officials within the party and the state apparatus. Zhdanov, for example, relied heavily on the full-time party officials of the central and local secretariat. Many of his Politburo allies also had strong party ties. Andreev had been a Central Committee Secretary for 11 years before he became Chairman of the Council on Kolkhoz Affairs in 1946. Khrushchev had served long periods in both the Moscow and Ukrainian party organisations. It was he who came to head the party soon after Stalin's death. The Zhdanov faction thus had particular support amongst several regional party organisations – in Zhdanov's own Leningrad as well as in the

Ukraine and Moscow (where another revivalist, G.M. Popov, was in charge in the 1940s).

In the main the state apparatus was the power base of Malenkov and Beria. However, Voznesenskii, Zhdanov's some-time ally, had many supporters within the Council of Ministers. His main base was the state planning agency, Gosplan, which he headed both before and during the war. He was one of eight deputy chairmen of the Council of Ministers in 1947 who held Politburo rank. Stalin was the chairman. Even in 1947, however, Voznesenskii and Andreev were outnumbered in the Council of Ministers by Malenkov, Beria, Voroshilov and Kaganovich.

The Malenkov Faction had their roots firmly in the state apparatus. In spite of a long career in the Central Committee Secretariat, Malenkov seemed to enjoy most support amongst the economic ministries. It was no accident that after Stalin's death, when forced to choose between party and state, he chose to head the Council of Ministers rather than become First Secretary of the party. Under his guidance the party revival of 1943–47 had been stopped and the power of the economic ministries reasserted in spite of the fact that Malenkov was in control of the Secretariat from late in 1948.

Beria's source of support lay in the police network, the Ministries of Internal Affairs and of State Security, and in his native Georgia. Stalin attacked both these bases in 1951. Besides the Mingrelian Affair the leader arranged for Beria's Minister of State Security, V.S. Avakumov, to be replaced by S.D. Ignatev who had stronger links with Khrushchev. As soon as Stalin died Beria himself replaced Ignatev and reunited the MGB with the MVD. His control over the police gave him two important advantages in the power game: fear and information. Although the MGB were kept more in check in the 1940s than they had been in 1935–38, there was always a possibility that Beria's men could be used against even the highest party and state officials as they had been during the Yezhovshchina. The MGB also provided Beria with information via an enormous network of informers at home and abroad. The breadth of his sources, encompassing all policy spheres, contrasted with the limited scope of knowledge gathering by individual ministries or party departments.

Of Malenkov and Beria's allies in the Politburo Kaganovich had strong ties with Khrushchev. However since 1935 he had worked mainly in the economic ministries. This was except for a few months in 1947 when Khrushchev was temporarily down-graded in the Ukraine and Kaganovich took over his post. Kaganovich had long been a hatchet man for Stalin. This was his function in the Ukraine in 1947, to check on Khrushchev's liberalism. Kaganovich's alliance with Malenkov and Beria was not always a happy one. Voroshilov, another Malenkov ally, had been posted to Hungary in 1945 but returned to Moscow in 1947 to work in the Council of Ministers.

The conflict of 1945–53 thus had all the air of party-state battles. This did not mean that Malenkov had no allies in the Secretariat nor that Zhdanov or Khrushchev had no supporters in the Council of Ministers. Neither was a completely united organisation. In any case alliances shifted. For example, Kaganovich supported Malenkov in arguments over reparation in 1945/46. Yet he seems to have aided Stalin's moves against Beria in 1951–52 and certainly backed Khrushchev's camp against the secret police chief after Stalin's death. Voznesenskii also seems to have backed Zhdanov on some issues and not others. there is no reason to suppose that any one of these factions was always united or that any of them had a permanent majority on the Politburo.

POLITICS BEYOND THE POLITBURO

From what has already been presented in these pages it is obvious that many of the party and state organisations described in Chapter 2 had an impact on the policy-making process. Their views influenced those of various Politburo members and they had varying degrees of impact on the implementation of the Politburo's decisions.

The production branch ministries had a substantial effect on policies in both industry and agriculture. In spite of their ties to Politburo members like Malenkov and Kaganovich their influence on the formation of policy was limited. Voznesenskii's Gosplan had at least as much and probably more impact on the setting out of policy priorities in plans and decrees. The ministries' power rested in their ability to divert resources into channels favoured by themselves rather than by the planners and the politicians. Their actions had the cumulative effect of starving the consumer goods industries, the eastern areas and the agricultural sector in particular of vital resources. Of course all supplies everywhere were in short supply after the war but heavy industry and the central economic region certainly suffered less from these shortages than their rivals. The result was that they fulfilled and overfulfilled their output targets to an extent that light industry, the east and agriculture could not achieve.

In foreign policy and culture the state apparatus was much more of a willing tool of the party and the leadership. In these spheres the ministries and committees of the Council of Ministers had little advantage in numbers and specialism over their checking rivals. The number of officials involved in foreign policy making was necessariy limited and so more easily checked upon than were millions of employees of industrial and agricultural ministries each with their own narrow field of specialism. In cultural affairs in many ways the party were the specialists. It was in the Secretariat's Agitprop department that the will of Marx, Lenin and Stalin was translated into dictates that were clear enough to be enforced at most levels.

The power of the ministries over the economy owes much to the weakness of the checking organs in this sphere. In spite of the party revival, party secretaries and their staff could not cope with the workload in dealing with hundreds of factories and farms in each area. In foreign affairs it was only the specialised departments within the Central Committee Secretariat in Moscow that were involved; in the sphere of culture the party apparatus was really the implementor rather than the checker. Decrees on cultural matters were issued by the Central Committee of the party and carried out by the Secretariat at all levels. At this time the Council of Ministers did not have a separate Ministry of Culture. In industry and agriculture plans were announced by the Council of Ministers and executed by dozens of ministries. The party's control over culture thus reinforces rather than contradicts the theory that it was the implementing bodies that exercised more influence over policy than their checkers in the USSR in the post-war decade. In many ways the party revival was most successful in culture and foreign policy where ministerial power was limited even before the revival began.

Of the other checking organs the Soviets' and the unions' impact was marginal. Deputies to the Supreme and local Soviets frequently complained about ministerial abuse and also sought to influence details of policy. There is little evidence, however, that much was done to remedy these shortcomings in the ministries' work. Neither was any basic policy decision ever amended to take account of the Soviets' views. Decrees were usually passed in its name by its own Presidium which was little more than a tool of the Politburo.

Of the unions it was only those involved in various spheres of culture that were involved to any degree in policy-making. Even then the Writers' and Composers' Unions tended to do what the Secretariat told them. This may have been in part because their leaders, men like Fadeev and Khremnikov, supported Zhdanov's hard line and were prepared after his demise to give their backing to Malenkov and Beria's new version of it. Certainly the membership of both of these elite unions did not take the Secretariat's attacks lying down. In the Institute of Economics as well as in these unions well-known artists and academics were allowed a surprising degree of freedom to voice their disapproval of new restrictions upon them. Several escaped anything more than public censure and survived until the tide turned again in their favour. A writer who refused to attend one of Zhdanov's meetings and an economist who refused to accept Ostrovityanov's formulas for research were not only allowed to go free but in some cases even got their views into print in the small circulation specialised press.

Debate and conflict within the artistic and academic elite was normally expected and allowed if it was kept within that circle even in Stalin's Russia. Lysenko's purge of biologists was the exception in its harshness rather than the rule at this time. The effectiveness of the debate in terms of its impact on policy depended very much, however, on the Politburo and ministerial/ Secretariat battles of the time. Artists and academicians were allowed a certain freedom of expression but they could be ignored by the leadership. Nevertheless they did generate ideas on profit incentives in industry, work organisation in agriculture, liberal- ism in writing and other spheres that came to fruition after 1953.

Of the checking organs within the Council of Ministers only the police had any real authority to oppose the party and the ministries. Apart from their role in the Leningrad and Anti- Cosmopolitan Affairs of 1943 the MGB and MVD kept a fairly low profile in Staln's last decade. Their main potential use was to check on the ministries. Yet the security of tenure enjoyed within the economic ministries shows that the police were not effectively fulfilling their role. The most likely explanation lies in the alliance between the chiefs of the two bodies, Malenkov and Beria. the MGB apparatus was used against foreign communists, against party officials in Leningrad and against writers and critics accused of cosmopolitanism. It was never used in any concerted attack on Malenkov's economic ministries.

MODELS OF SOVIET POLITICS AND THE POST-WAR DECADE

In Chapter 1 we outlined three models of the Soviet policy-making process: the totalitarian, the bureaucratic and the pluralist. None of these models in either its original or its modified form provides a completely accurate picture of the process in all the policy spheres we have discussed. Even if we adapt the totalitarian theory to encompass conflict within the Politburo it cannot account for the policy debates conducted amongst economists and planners nor can it deal with the impact of the ministries on the implementation of policy. The bureaucratic model does allow for such features but may understate their influence on industrial and agricultural policy. The leadership, or at least a majority in it, wanted further development in the eastern regions and a new boost for light industry and agriculture. They were denied this by the actions of the ministerial bureaucracy. The pluralist model in its modified form can explain this powerlessness.

Yet both the bureaucratic and the pluralist models seriously overemphasise involvement of non-Politburo officials in the making of foreign and cultural policy. There were bureaucratic and pluralist tendencies in both these policy spheres. For example, communists in other countries tended to interpret Moscow's foreign-policy directives in their own way and writers often sought to limit the Secretariat's restrictions upon them. These influences were, however, minor compared to the changing balance of power within the Politburo. The "conflict" version of the totalitarian model provides a good explanation of the changes in foreign and cultural policy from 1946 to 1948. For example both the August 1946 decree that marked the start of the Zhdanov-shchina and the later communisation of Eastern Europe were primarily the result of the changing balance of power within the Politburo.

The pluralist model therefore comes closest to describing industrial and agricultural policy-making although only in its modified form which brings it closer to the bureaucratic model. The totalitarian conflict theory is the best explanation of foreign policy but there were significant bureaucratic elements in it, especially within the cultural sphere seems the most totalitarian of all. Yet even there, writers and composers attempted some resistance to the party's power, a resistance which was rewarded by the more liberal attitudes of the early 1950s.

No one model can accurately describe the political process of Stalin's last decade in all policy spheres. Each one highlights certain features that are crucial to the explanation of why some policies turned out as they did. However the extremes of personal glorification of Stalin that made up the personality cult did not describe the policy process in most spheres with any accuracy. At the very least the rest of the Politburo had some influence over Stalin.

THE ORIGINS OF THE THAW

In all the policy spheres analysed in this book great changes were wrought within five years of Stalin's death. It is often assumed that discussion of these reforms was banned before 1953. Although Stalin may have blacked some of the reforms (for example, abolition of the MTSy) he appears to have allowed discussion of most of them before his death. The thaw of 1953–58 presided over by Khrushchev, and to some extent Malenkov, had already begun in Stalin's declining years.

In the industrial sphere the problems of regionalisation and the power of the central ministries dragged on until 1957 when Khrushchev abolished the latter and replaced them with regional economic councils (*Sovnarkhozy*). Even then the old system was reintroduced after his removal in 1964. The attempt to revive the consumer goods sector was revived by Malenkov in 1954. It is noteworthy, however, that as late as 1975 attempts to boost light industrial output were failing due to the power of the heavy industrial ministries.[4] It was Khrushchev who ordered a drive to boost the technically advanced new industries like chemicals that had been neglected during the period 1945–53. All these policies had been discussed during Stalin's last decade.

In agriculture Khrushchev had long been advocating a new approach based on giving the *Kolkhoznik* more incentive to work harder by paying him more for his produce and giving him better living conditions. In September 1953 he was able to make a start at putting his ideas into practice. A Central Committee plenum in that month heard his report detailing the problems of the agricultural sector and approved his reforms.

Two other major reforms in Soviet agricultural administration which had been discussed (and in one case adopted for a time) during Stalin's last decade were introduced by Khrushchev in 1958. The link system abolished in 1950 was revived as a large-scale experiment with the First Secretary's backing. It also took on a more extreme form than in Andreev's day. Links were allowed in some areas to work the same plot of land for an entire crop cycle and even to own or control the machinery with which they worked it. This covert revival of private agriculture (as its opponents described it in the late 1950s and 1960s) was made possible by the abolition of the MTS system in 1958. What Sanina and Venzher had advocated under Stalin became a reality less than a decade later, thus allowing collective farms and links to operate their own machinery.

In foreign policy Khrushchev's thaw was linked to the policy of peaceful coexistence with the West. Yet not only was this peace line advocated by Stalin's leadership as early as 1951,[5] but Khrushchev's policies also echoed those of Stalin in 1945/46. In 1956 Khrushchev talked of peaceful competition between capitalism and communism and of "different paths to socialism". In 1945 Stalin had told Djilas that socialism was possible under an English king. He also told Mikolajczyk, of the Polish exile government in London in 1944, "communism fits Germany as a saddle fits a cow".[6] The same views that prompted the Politburo to send a high-ranking delegation to Paris to discuss possible Soviet *acceptance* of Marshall aid in 1947 was behind Khrushchev's policies of a decade later.

In the sphere of cultural policy we have already seen how moves were set afoot in 1951 to ease restrictions on writers. Whatever the motives for these steps they set in motion a process that led to further liberalisation from 1954 and culminated in Khrushchev's decision to publish Solzhenitzyn's novel about Stalin's prison camps *One Day in the Life of Ivan Denisovich*. Indeed the man who pressed for that publication, Aleksandr Tvardovsky, had been appointed editor of the journal *Novy Mir* which published Solzhenitzyn's work some three years *before* Stalin's death.

Even the Khrushchev-inspired moves to limit the power of the secret police were merely an adaptation of policies initiated by Stalin himself. By dividing the NKVD into two ministries in 1943 and removing some of Beria's supporters from the MGB in 1951, Stalin was beginning the policies that Khrushchev brought to a climax in September 1953 with the arrest of Beria.

All this does not show that Khrushchev was continuing Stalin's policies. Many of his innovations had been rejected by the 1945–53 Politburo. The point is that 1953 was not quite such a sudden turning point in Soviet history as Khrushchev himself would have had us believe in his de-Stalinisation campaigns. The policies of 1953–63 had mostly been under discussion for several years before Stalin's death and in some cases had even formed a part of Politburo policy under the Generalissimo himself.

Notes

CHAPTER 1: SOVIET POLITICS IN STALIN'S LAST DECADE

1. R.W. Pethybridge, *A History of Post-War Russia* (London: Allen & Unwin, 1966) p. 15.
2. W.O. McCagg Jr, *Stalin Embattled 1943–48* (Detroit: Wayne State University Press, 1978) and M. Shulman, *Stalin's Foreign Policy Reappraised* (Cambridge, Mass.: Harvard UP, 1963).
3. V.S. Dunham, *In Stalin's Time: Middle Class Values in Soviet Fiction* (Cambridge UP, 1976).
4. A. Werth, *Russia: the Post-War Years* (London: Robert Hale, 1971). Unfortunately the author's account ends in 1948; his untimely death prevented any account of Stalin's last five years. W.G. Hahn, *Post-War Soviet Politics: the Fall of Zhdanov and the Defeat of Moderation 1946–53* (Ithaca, N.Y.: Cornell UP, 1982) concentrates on particular episodes without attempting to give an overall picture of the period.
5. The most valuable of these are: R. Conquest, *Power and Policy in the USSR* (London: Macmillan, 1961); Pethybridge, op. cit.; M. Fainsod, *How Russia is Ruled* (Cambridge, Mass.: Harvard UP, 1961); L. Shapiro, *The Communist Party of the Soviet Union* (London: Methuen, 1963).
6. Introduction to Dunham, op. cit., p. xii.
7. *Planovoe Khozyaistvo*, no. 2 (Moscow: Gosplanizdat, 1947) p. 84.
8. S.I. Ploss, *Conflict and Decision-Making in Soviet Russia: a Case Study of Agricultural Policy 1953–63* (Princeton UP, 1969) pp. 10–23.
9. A. Inkeles, *Social Change in Soviet Russia* (Cambridge, Mass.: Harvard UP, 1968) ch. 15.
10. See for example, *Khrushchev Remembers*, vol. 1 (includes "secret speech"), (Sphere Books, 1971).
11. A.G. Zverev, *Zapiski Ministra* (Moscow: Politizdat, 1973); I.G. Erenburg, *Post-War Years 1945–54* (London: MacGibbon & Kee, 1966).
12. For example, V.V. Kolotov, *Nikolai Alekseevich Voznesenskii* (Moscow: Politizdat, 1974).
13. See for example *Narodnoe Khozyaistvo SSSR* (annually since 1956) (Moscow: 1957–); *Kapital'noe Stroitel'stvo V SSSR* (Moscow, 1961); *Trud V SSSR* (Moscow, 1967).
14. For a detailed discussion of the utility of these statistics see T. Dunmore, *The Stalinist Command Economy* (London: Macmillan, 1980) Appendix A, pp. 149–50.
15. See, for example, *Resheniya Partii i Pravtel'stva po Khozyaistvennym Voprosam Tom 3* (1941–52 gody) (Moscow, Politizdat, 1968), (hereafter "*Resheniya*"). *KPSS*

V Rezolyutsiakh i Resheniyakh Tom 6 (Moscow, Politizdat, 1968) (hereafter "*KPSS*").

16. See Yu.A. Prikhod′ko, *Vosstanovlenie Industrii 1942–50* (Moscow: Mysl′, 1973); M.A. Dvoinishnikov, *Deyaltel′nost′ KPSS po Vosstanovleniyu Promyshlennosti V Poslevoennoi Period* (Moscow: Politizdat, 1977); B.Z. Zagitov, "Nekotorye Voprosy Partiinogo Stoitel′strva V Pervye Poslevoennye gody (1945–50)" in *Voprosy Partiinoi Raboty na Sovremennoi Etape* (Moscow: Mysl′, 1969).

17. See McCagg, op. cit.; Hahn, op. cit.; Dunmore op. cit.

18. D. Tarschys, "The Soviet Political System: Three Models", *European Journal of Political Science*, no. 5, 1977, pp. 287–320.

19. This is the term used by T.H. Rigby, "Traditional Market and Organizational Societies and the USSR", *World Politics*, no. 4, 1964.

20. See C.J. Friedrich and Z.K. Brzezinski, *Totalitarian Dictatorship and Autocracy* (Cambridge, Mass.: Harvard UP, 1956).

21. See Conquest, op. cit., *passim*.

22. The term can be found in Carl Linden, *Khrushchev and the Soviet Leadership* (Baltimore, 1966).

23. See below chs 3–76.

24. See, for example, T.H. Rigby, "Traditional, Market and Organisational Societies", *World Politics* 1963/64, pp. 539–57.

CHAPTER 2:   THE SOVIET POWER STRUCTURE, 1945–53

1. M. Djilas, *Conversations with Stalin* (London: Hart-Davis, 1962) p. 134.

2. *Khrushchev Remembers*, *passim*.

3. Ibid., p. 248.

4. *Plenum Tsentral′nogo Komiteta Kommunisticheskoi Partii Sovetskoyo Soyuza 18–21 Iyunya 1963g. Stenograficheskii otchet* (Moscow: 1963) p. 289 (hereafter *Plenum*).

5. R. Medvedev, *Let History Judge* (London: Macmillan, 1972) p. 557.

6. Ibid., p. 490.

7. *Plenum*, p. 280.

8. *Khrushchev Remembers*, Vol. 1, p. 554 (reprint of "Secret Speech").

9. Werth, op. cit., p. 283.

10. For a brief survey of these disputes see Dunmore, op. cit., pp. 2–3. The themes dealt with here will be discussed in more detail in later chapters.

11. McCagg, op. cit., ch. 14.

12. A 1951 purge of officials in Beria's native Georgia, many of whom were allies of his (for a fuller account see Conquest, op. cit., ch. 7).

13. A. Nove, *An Economic History of the USSR* (Harmondsworth: Penguin, 1969) p. 294; the secretaries who were not Politburo members are also included for the sake of completeness. Their status was probably less than that of candidate members of the Politburo.

14. The reference here is to the 19th Party Congress at which the creation of a new enlarged Politburo (to be called the Presidium) was announced. This was used to remove one or two Politburo members and to transfer others in order to break up the loyalties being analysed in this section, and arguably to prepare the ground for further dismissals.

15. See J. Hough, "The Soviet Concept of the Relationship Between the Lower Party Organs and the State Administration", in J.L. Nogee (ed.), *Man, State, and Society in the Soviet Union* (London: Pall Mall Press, 1972) pp. 142–46.
16. See Dunmore, op. cit., pp. 6–8.
17. This structure applied to all ministries at the time, see A.Y. Vyshinsky (ed.), *The Law of the Soviet State* (New York: Macmillan, 1948) p. 388.
18. Dunmore, op. cit., pp. 10–11. Such "reinterpretation" was formally illegal (see Vyshinsky, p. 416) but frequently practised.
19. Three other ministries (those of Procurement, Material Reserves and Trade) do not fall easily into either category. Their involvement in trade gave them both administrative and checking functions (e.g. the Ministry of Procurement helped to check that collective farms were growing the right crops in the right quantities).
20. S.A. Akopov; A.I. Kostousov; V.A. Malyshev; N.K. Baybakov; D.F. Ustinov; A.N. Kosygin; A.A. Ishkov.
21. See McCagg, op. cit., pp. 89–90; he interprets the reorganising of the industrial ministries in 1945/46 as an (unsuccessful) attempt to break the power of what he calls the "managers". However, most of these reorganisations seem merely to reflect the transition to a civilian economy (see note 22 below).
22. For example P.I. Parshin had been Minister of Mortar Production during the war. In February 1946 his ministry was renamed that of Machine Building and Instrument Manufacture. He remained at the head of this ministry until it was abolished after Stalin's death.
23. Formerly the Ministry of the Armed Forces.
24. See M. Kolosov, *Kommunisticheskaya Partiya i Sovetskaya Armiya* (München: Institut po Izucheniya istorii i Kultury SSSR, 1954).
25. *The Land of Socialism Today and Tomorrow* (Report of the 18th Congress of the CPSU (B), Moscow, Foreign Languages Publishing House, 1939) pp. 449 ff.
26. For a fuller account of both attempts see Conquest, op. cit. chs 7 and 8.
27. Werth, op. cit., p. 35.
28. See above, pp. 22–3.
29. See Dunmore, op. cit., pp. 20–1.
30. Vyshinsky, op. cit., p. 380.
31. See Dunmore, op. cit., pp. 19–20 and 88–9.
32. L. Shapiro, op. cit., pp. 526–27.
33. Ibid., p. 525n.
34. J. Hough, *The Soviet Prefects: the Local Party Organs in Industrial Decision-Making* (Cambridge, Mass.: Harvard UP, 1968).
35. *Pravda*, 27 December 1946, p. 1.
36. *Naglyadnoe Posobie po partinnomy stroitelstvom* (Moscow, 1970) p. 24.
37. *The Land of Socialism Today & Tomorrow*, p. 463.
38. Dunmore, op. cit., p. 18.
39. *The Land of Socialism Today and Tomorrow*, p. 463.
40. Dunham, op. cit., p. 12.
41. B.Z. Zagitov, op. cit., p. 225.
42. Ibid., p. 226.

43. See *History of the Communist Party of the Soviet Union* (Moscow, 1960) pp. 626–30 and "*KPSS*", pp. 180–9 and 277–80.
44. Zagitov, op. cit., p. 239.
45. The figure of 58 000 new admissions from January 1947 to October 1952 compares very closely to the *net* increase in membership of 655 638 from January 1947 to January 1953. T.H. Rigby, *Communist Party Membership in the USSR 1917–67* (Princeton: Princeton UP, 1968) estimates expulsions from 1951–53 at 10 000 p.a. This may well be an overestimate. Even so, it represents a "purge" rate of only about 1.5 per cent p.a.
46. Vyshinsky, op. cit., p. 623.
47. A.P. Efimov, *Pravda*, 2 February 1951, p. 2.

CHAPTER 3: INDUSTRIAL POLICY

1. For a fuller evaluation of the evacuation and the impact of new investment see Dunmore, op. cit., pp. 33–42.
2. Data from *Sbornik Soobshchennii Chrezvychinoi Gosudarstvennoi Komm sii o Zlodeyaniyakh Nemetsko-Fashistikikh Zakhvatchikov* (Moscow, 1946) pp. 428–57.
3. (Report of the Soviet Reparations Committee), that is, produced in the Trans-Volga, Urals, West and East Siberian and Far Eastern economic regions of the RSFSR and in the Central Asian republic.
4. For a comment on the reliability of these statistics see Dunmore, op. cit., Appendix A, pp. 149–50.
5. See *Pravda*, 9 February and 8 February 1946.
6. *Bol'shevik*, no. 21, 1945, pp. 1–13 (Molotov's speech) and pp. 14–19 (editorial commentary on it).
7. For a fuller account see Dunmore, op. cit., pp. 42–54.
8. For example, the Smolensk oblast', part of the Russian republic, was included in the same economic region as the Belorussian republic.
9. Voznesenskii may of course have had second thoughts on the issue, but only because of the pressure of the complex development faction.
10. See for example the article by Granovskii in *Bol'shevik*, no. 13, 1945, pp. 23–36 and by Zelenovskii in *Planovoe Khozyaistvo*, no. 1, 1946, pp. 67–79. These journals were published in editions of only one or two thousand.
11. For more detailed analysis of the plan's regional implications see Dunmore, op. cit., pp. 45–52.
12. For more detail see ibid., ch. 4.
13. Ibid., pp. 54–61.
14. *Planovoe Khozyaistvo*, no. 3, 1947, p. 5.
15. A. Korobov, *Planovoe Khozyaistvo*, no. 3, 1946, p. 20.
16. I. Kuzminov, *Bol'shevik*, nos. 17–18, 1945, p. 35.
17. A.G. Zverev, op. cit., pp. 227–30.
18. In 1947 both wages and prices were revalued by ten times, whilst savings remained at their old levels.
19. See Dunmore, op. cit., pp. 112–14.
20. *Bol'shevik*, no. 21, 1945, p. 14.
21. See Dunmore, op. cit., p. 100.

22. The following account is a summary of a more detailed analysis presented in ibid., ch. 5.
23. *Planovoe Khozyaistvo*, no. 4, 1946, p. 4.
24. A. Petrov, ibid., no. 2, 1947, pp. 58 and 66.
25. Dunmore, op. cit., p. 112.
26. M. Djilas, op. cit.
27. For a more detailed summary and references see Dunmore, op. cit., pp. 59–61 and 113.
28. J.V. Stalin, *Ekonomicheskie Problemy Sotsializma v SSSR* (Moscow, Gospolitizdat, 1952) pp. 55–6.

CHAPTER 4: AGRICULTURAL POLICY

1. L. Volin, *A Survey of Russian Agriculture* (US Dept. of Agriculture, 1951) p. 20.
2. *Narodnoe Khozyaistvo SSSR 1922–72* (Statistika, Moscow, 1972) p. 216.
3. See *Resheniya*, Tom 3, pp. 336–41.
4. Ibid., p. 407.
5. R.F. Miller, *One Hundred Thousand Tractors* (Cambridge, Mass., Harvard UP, 1970) pp. 282–3.
6. *Resheniya*, Tom 3, p. 490.
7. Ibid., pp. 531–49. Note that in this 1968 edition all mention of Stalin is omitted.
8. See V.N. Sukachev, *Stalinskii Plan Preobrazovaniya Prirody* (Moscow, Akademia Nank SSSR, 1950) p. 14.
9. See ibid., *passim*.
10. *Sel'skoe Khozyaistvo SSSR* (M. Statistika, 1971) p. 245 (hereafter *SKh*); *Resheniya*, Tom 3.
11. *Khrushchev Remembers*, pp. 201–15.
12. Ibid., p. 207.
13. *SKh*. Grain statistics are given as biological yield less 20 per cent to give the more accurate barn yield (see N. Jasny, *The Socialized Agriculture of the USSR* (Stanford, UP, 1949) pp. 728–36. Output plans for other sectors have not been discounted. If they were, it would still mean that only one more target (that for sugar beet) would have been achieved.
14. All data in this paragraph from *SKh*.
15. See the plan fulfilment reports published in *Pravda* in January 1951 and 1952.
16. *SKh*.
17. *SKh*.
18. See for example, P. Doronin in *Partiinaya Zhizn'*, no. 17, 1947, p. 14.
19. F. Belov, *The History of a Soviet Collective Farm* (New York, Praeger, 1955) pp. 16–24.
20. Ibid., pp. 130–1.
21. Doronin, op. cit., pp. 6–15.
22. They were, for example, allotted their plots of land for only one year instead of an entire crop cycle.
23. For example, they were allowed to grow several crops, rather like a complete farm.

24. J. Stalin, *Ekonomicheskie Problemy*, pp. 84–94.
25. See for example the novel by V. Ovechkin, *Raionnye Budni* in *Dorogi, Nami Razvedannye* (Moscow: Sovetskii Pisatel', 1967) pp. 128–494.
26. See *Pravda*, 4 March 1950. The following day's issue carried a note to the effect that the article had been "for discussion purposes only" and had not become official policy.
27. *Khrushchev Remembers*, pp. 209–10.
28. Belov, op. cit., p. 145.
29. Ibid., p. 144.

CHAPTER 5: FOREIGN POLICY

1. See, for example, the works cited above by Shulman, McCagg, Werth and Pethybridge and H. Seton-Watson, *The Pattern of Communist Revolutions*.
2. For a succinct summary of his argument see Seton-Watson, op. cit.
3. See, for example, Werth, op. cit., Introduction.
4. Quoted in Werth, op. cit., p. 251.
5. See L. Schapiro, *The CPSU*, pp. 507–8.
6. J.P. Nettl, *The Eastern Zone and Soviet Policy in Germany 1945–50* (Oxford: OUP, 1951) p. 202.
7. I. Deutscher, *Stalin* (London: Penguin, 1966) pp. 522–3.
8. Nettl, op. cit., pp. 219–20.
9. McCagg, op. cit., especially ch. 1.
10. Nettl, op. cit., p. 81.
11. His name ceased to appear on official listings; see Hahn, op. cit., p. 102.
12. This may explain why Hahn sees Zhdanov as more of a moderate than the insurrectionist image attached to him by McCagg. Allowing different routes to and forms of socialism in other states has always been a liberal position in Soviet politics.
13. For a clear account of this and subsequent manoeuvres see Hahn, op. cit. pp. 99–102. See also Djilas, op. cit., *passim*.
14. T. Wittlin, *Commissar: The Life and Death of Lavrenty Pavlovich Beria* (London: Angus & Robertson, 1973).
15. See above, pp. 90–1.
16. Shulman, op. cit., ch. 1.
17. Quoted in op. cit., p. 31.

CHAPTER 6: CULTURAL POLICY

1. Quoted in Werth, op. cit., p. 99.
2. See H. Swayze, *Political Control of Literature in the USSR* (Cambridge, Mass., Harvard UP, 1962) pp. 29–32 ff.
3. Quoted in ibid., p. 36.
4. Quoted in Werth, p. 206.
5. "O. Zhurnalakh 'Zvezda' i 'Leningrad'," in *O Partiinoi i Sovetskoi Pechati, Radio Veshchanii i Televidenii* (Moscow: Mysl', 1972) p. 259.
6. Hahn, op. cit.

7. See Werth, op. cit., p. 210.
8. Ibid., pp. 373–5.
9. See W.N. Vickery, "Zhdanovism (1946–53)", in Hayward and L. Labedz· (eds), *Literature and Revolution in Soviet Russia* (London: OUP, 1963) pp. 114–5.
10. See ibid., pp. 105–6.
11. See *OP*, pp. 271–7.
12. Ibid., p. 276.
13. See Swayze op. cit., pp. 75–6 and Vickery, op. cit., pp. 111–14.
14. E.g., see E.R. Frankel, *Novy Mir: a Case Study in the Politics of Literature 1952–58* (London: Cambridge UP, 1981) pp. 4–19.
15. Swayze, op. cit., p. 64.
16. For a fuller account see Conquest, op. cit., ch. 7.
17. Swayze, pp. 64–5.
18. Ibid., p. 69; RAPP was the Russian Association of Proletarian writers. Founded in 1925, it was a party-backed movement aimed at the proletarianisation of Soviet literature.
19. *Pravda*, 30 March 1950.
20. See Frankel, op. cit., p. 10.
21. See the quotes from Ilya Ehrenburg's memoirs in ibid., p. 12.
22. L. Gruliow (ed.), *Current Soviet Politics: Documentary Record of 19th Party Congress* (NY: Praeger, 1953).
23. See McCagg, op. cit., p. 203 and note 63, p. 378.
24. See Hahn, p. 95.
25. *OP*, pp. 428–9.
26. For a fuller account see Hahn, p. 111.
27. See Swayze, op. cit., p. 73.
28. *OP*, pp. 435 ff.

CHAPTER 7:   CONCLUSION

1. See Conquest, op. cit., *passim*.
2. See above note 26 to ch. 3.
3. This is the view of both Hahn and McCagg; yet both were promoted in 1948 at a time when Zhdanov's fortunes were ebbing.
4. The Ninth Five Year Plan (1971–75) envisaged a faster growth rate for heavy than light industry. Yet heavy industry still grew faster in the end!
5. See Shulman, op. cit., introduction.
6. Quoted in Deutscher, op. cit., p. 527.

Index